Excel

Revise in a Month

Year 3
NAPLAN*-style Tests

PASCAL
PRESS

* This is not an officially endorsed publication of the NAPLAN program and is produced by Pascal Press independently of Australian governments.

Alan Horsfield & Allyn Jones

Revised in 2011 for NAPLAN Test changes—new Reading question formats and new Writing Test (persuasive texts)

Reprinted 2011 (twice), 2012
New NAPLAN Test question formats added 2012
Reprinted 2014, 2015

ISBN 978 1 74125 207 1

Pascal Press
PO Box 250
Glebe NSW 2037
(02) 8585 4044
www.pascalpress.com.au

Publisher: Vivienne Joannou
Project editors: Fiona Sim and Mark Dixon
Edited by Fiona Sim and Mark Dixon
Answers checked by Peter Little, Dale Little, Elaine Horsfield and Carolyn Lain
Typeset by Precision Typesetting (Barbara Nilsson)
Cover and page design by DiZign Pty Ltd
Printed by Green Giant Press

Acknowledgements
Barry, Bill, *Before Computers*, HBJ, Sydney, 1990
Chionh, Ida, *Celebrations*, HBJ, Sydney, 1990
Chionh, Ida, *Do you speak English?*, HBJ, Sydney, 1989
Dalgleish, Joan, *Dog on a Diet*, HBJ, Sydney, 1989
Deacon, Christine, *Pandas*, HBJ, Sydney, 1990
Hooper, Carole, *Puppets*, HBJ, Sydney, 1990
Horsfield, Alan, 'Fearless Brian', adapted from version in *Dreams*, Ginninderra Press, Canberra, 2002
Horsfield, Alan, 'Fancy Dress Party', unpublished
Horsfield, Alan, 'Simon's Solution', unpublished
Horsfield, Alan, 'The Wind and the Sun', unpublished
Horsfield, Elaine, 'Clean Your Room!', in *Kids' Stuff*, Peranga Post Publishers, Peranga (Qld), 2005
Horsfield, Elaine, 'My Cat', unpublished
Horsfield, Elaine, 'Quiet Please!', in *Kids' Stuff*, Peranga Post Publishers, Peranga (Qld), 2005
Jarman-Walker, Jenny, *My Diary*, HBJ, Sydney, 1990
Sloan, Peter and Latham, Ross, *Animal Reports*, HBJ, Sydney, 1989
Power, Shane, *Hearty Facts*, HBJ, Sydney, 1990
Wright, Viki, *The Tooth Book*, HBJ, Sydney, 1990

Photograph on page 62 by photos.com
Bubble Busters back cover, page 82, reproduced courtesy of Blake Publishing
Photograph on page 19 by David Atkinson, www.minyos.its.rmit.edu.au/~dwa/WayangKulit.html. Reproduced with permission.

NAPLAN is a trademark of Australian Curriculum, Assessment and Reporting Authority (ACARA).

All efforts have been made to obtain permission for the copyright material reproduced in this book. In the event of any oversight, the publisher welcomes any information that will enable rectification of any reference or credit in subsequent editions.

Table of Contents

The NAPLAN Tests

Introduction

NAPLAN stands for National Assessment Program—Literacy and Numeracy. See the official NAPLAN website (www.naplan.edu.au) for more details.

In 2008 Australian students in Years 3, 5, 7 and 9 were tested for the first time on aspects of literacy and numeracy using the same year level tests. The types of test questions and the test formats used were familiar to teachers and students.

Tests are held in mid-May each year. The test results are used by teachers as a diagnostic tool. The results provide students, parents and teachers with information that can be used to improve student learning.

The Student Report provides information about what students know and can do in the areas of Reading, Writing, Language Conventions (Spelling, Punctuation and Grammar) and the various strands of Numeracy. It also provides information on how each student has performed in relation to other students in his or her year group, and against the national average and the national minimum standard.

Naplan Tests are not aptitude or intelligence tests. They focus on what has been achieved, especially on the knowledge and skills taught in the syllabus. These are often called KLAs (key learning areas).

Official tests are trialled on selected groups to test the reliability of the questions. The questions in this book are representative of questions that you can expect to find in an official test. They have been prepared by professionals who have an understanding of teaching and of testing procedures. There are more questions in this book than can be included in any test in any one year.

States and schools may also conduct their own tests independently of the NAPLAN program.

The NAPLAN Tests were originally developed by the Curriculum Corporation in conjunction with State and Territory Departments of Education or Boards of Studies and are now being developed by ACARA (Australian Curriculum, Assessment and Reporting Authority).

The *My School* website

The NAPLAN results present an objective view of student performance and form the basis from which schools can make informed educational decisions about further school learning programs.

Because NAPLAN Tests are national tests they provide authorities with sufficient information to track student educational development from primary to high school, or when transferring from one Australian school to another.

The *My School* website (www.myschool.edu.au) provides NAPLAN results for most Australian schools. The site's Frequently Asked Questions (FAQs) will answer most questions about NAPLAN.

Areas assessed

The tests assess two basic Learning Areas: literacy and numeracy.

The Literacy Tests focus on:
- reading and comprehension of different types of information from stories and articles
- the correct use of language—especially spelling, punctuation and grammar
- writing types of texts such as a persuasive text, a narrative text or a recount text.

The Numeracy Tests focus on:
- ◎ the basic number skills of addition, subtraction, multiplication and division
- ◎ knowledge of some fractions and decimals, but also percentages, shapes and measurements
- ◎ interpretation of data contained in charts and graphs.

There are many different aspects of literacy and numeracy and the tests emphasise only some aspects. This book provides examples of questions based on a larger number of strands than could be expected to be assessed in a single paper.

Preparing for the tests

Most questions are multiple choice but some require students to express their answer in different ways. Students may be asked to order a sequence by using the numbers 1 to 4. There is also a writing component that is graded and marked by a special team of markers. There are time limits for each test. These are usually set so that almost everyone can complete the tests in the time allowed. There will also be a rest break between tests.

The official tests are held on three separate days and are well organised. Teachers will give children practice tests in the weeks before the NAPLAN Tests. Pupils will be shown how to complete the information on the cover of the tests and how to record their answers. Teachers receive special instructions for administering the tests.

Using this book

This book is designed to be used over four weeks, with weekly exercises in various aspects of literacy and numeracy. Each session gives students an opportunity to Test their Skills, revise Key Points and practise a Real Test on a specific aspect of the curriculum. In a month the student will have covered much of the material that could be included in a NAPLAN Test. Finally, there are two Sample Test Papers based on the format used in past Test Papers. Read *Follow this plan to revise for the Year 3 NAPLAN Tests!* on pages vi and vii for the recommended method of using this book.

Because NAPLAN Tests are timed tests, times have been suggested for completing the various units in this book. Students do not need rulers, white out, biros or calculators.

Types of tests

There are four different types of tests in Year 3 NAPLAN.

1 The Numeracy Test (45 minutes)

2 The Language Conventions Test (40 minutes)

3 The Reading Test (45 minutes)

4 The Writing Test (40 minutes)

Note: Tests 2–4 form the Literacy component of the test.

The Language Conventions Test and Writing Test are held on the first day, the Reading Test on the second day and the Numeracy Test on the last day.

Follow this plan to revise for the Year 3 NAPLAN Tests!

Selecting Topics

The maximum number of topics is given for each day. Students do not need to complete every topic—they should choose the topics that they need to practise.

Each student will take a different time to complete the topic, depending on their ability. The times given are **suggested times only**.

In Each Week

Day 1

On Day 1 there are **two topics in Mathematics** to prepare you for the Numeracy Test. For example, Week 1 Day 1 has the choice of these topics:

◎ Number and Algebra: Whole numbers, addition and subtraction
◎ Number and Algebra: Multiplication and division.

Each topic has these parts to it:

◎ **Test Your Skills** allows you to test your skills on this topic. You should time yourself. Suggested time given on the clock at the top of the page is 20 minutes. When you have finished, check the answers at the bottom of the page. If you are unsure how the correct answer was reached, see the explanations at the back of the book.

◎ **Key Points** gives a summary of the topic. Read these if you did not understand any of the Test Your Skills questions.

◎ **Real Tests** allow you to answer questions like those in a real Numeracy Test, so they are harder than the ones on the Test Your Skills pages. Answers and explanations are given at the back of the book. Time yourself doing these questions. Suggested time given on the clock is 20 minutes, which is the same amount of time you would be given to complete the questions in the Numeracy Test.

Day 2

On Day 2 there are **two topics from Spelling and one topic from Grammar and Punctuation**. They are to prepare you for the Language Conventions Test. For example, Week 1 Day 2 covers:

◎ Spelling: Making plurals from nouns
◎ Spelling: Common misspellings
◎ Grammar and Punctuation: Types of sentences and articles.

Each topic has these parts:

◎ **Key Points** gives a summary of the topic. Read this for a quick revision of the topic.

◎ **Test Your Skills** allows you to test your skills on this topic. You should time yourself. Suggested time for reading the Key Points and doing the Test Your Skills questions is 15 minutes. Check your answers and re-read the Key Points above if any of your answers were incorrect.

◎ **Real Tests** allow you to answer questions like those in a real Language Conventions Test, so they are harder than the ones on the Test Your Skills pages. Time yourself doing these questions. Suggested time given on the clock is 15 minutes, which is the same amount of time you would be given to complete the questions in the Language Conventions Test. Answers and explanations are given at the back of the book.

Day 3

On Day 3 there are **four different reading texts to practise comprehension**. This is part of the Reading Test. The four texts are examples of particular types of texts. For example, Week 2 Day 3 covers:

◎ Interpreting visual texts
◎ Understanding poetry.

Each week has these parts:

◎ **Test Your Skills** allows you to revise the main characteristics of the type of text and then test your comprehension of an extract. You should time yourself. Suggested time given on the clock at the top of the page is between 6 and 8 minutes. You can check the answers at the bottom of the page. If you are unsure how the correct answer was reached, see the explanations at the back of the book.

◎ **Real Tests** allow you to answer questions like those in the real Reading Test, so they are harder than the ones in Test Your Skills. Time yourself doing these questions. Suggested time given on the clock is between 6 and 8 minutes, which is the same amount of time you would be given to complete the questions in the Reading Test. Answers and explanations are given at the back of the book.

Day 4

Day 4 deals with writing. Each week there are **four Writing Tests**. This is part of the Literacy Tests. You can choose one of the tests to practise your writing. For example, Week 4 Day 4 deals with:

◎ Description of a place or scene
◎ Description of a person
◎ Explanation.

Each weekly Writing section has these parts:

◎ Tips for writing a particular type of text, which tells you how to structure and organise your text.

◎ The **Real Tests** allow you to respond to questions like those in a real Writing Test. Different stimulus material is given for each exercise so that you can practise responding to a variety of stimulus types. Writing tips will help you get started. Time yourself. Suggested time given on the clock is 40 minutes, which is the same amount of time you would be given to complete the questions in the Writing Test. Marking guides are provided in the answers at the back of the book so that you can have your work checked.

In addition, on pages 20–21 **General Writing Tips** are provided. Read these through each week before you begin.

Sample Test Papers

◎ Two **Sample Test Papers** appear at the end of the book. They are very similar to the real Year 3 NAPLAN Tests.

◎ Before attempting the Sample Test Papers, make sure you have done the **Real Test** for any topic you were unsure of and that you have worked through the answers for any questions you answered incorrectly.

◎ The Sample Test Papers have been divided into four sessions like the real Year 3 NAPLAN Tests. Make sure you take a break between sessions. The Language Conventions Test and the Writing Test are in the first two sessions. The time allowed for each of these tests is 40 minutes. The Reading Test is in the third session and the Numeracy Test is in the last session. The time allowed for each of these tests is 45 minutes. The Sample Test Papers follow the format of the NAPLAN Tests.

◎ **Answers and explanations** for the Sample Test Papers are given at the back of the book, on pages 155–172.

Notes for parents and teachers

The topics covered in this guide are typical of the teaching program used in most schools. To encourage the development of numeracy skills, all questions can be undertaken without the use of a calculator.

Let's start to revise!

Week

1

This is what we cover this week:

Day 1 **Number and Algebra:** ◎ Whole numbers, addition and subtraction
◎ Multiplication and division

Day 2 **Spelling:** ◎ Making plurals from nouns
◎ Common misspellings

Grammar and Punctuation: ◎ Types of sentences and articles

Day 3 **Reading:** ◎ Understanding narratives

Day 4 **Writing:** ◎ Persuasive texts

Test Your Skills

NUMBER AND ALGEBRA
Whole numbers, addition and subtraction

20 MIN

Circle the correct answer.

1 What is the place value of 3 in 7 306?
- A units (ones)
- B tens
- C hundreds
- D thousands

2 What whole number comes just before 40?
- A 30
- B 39
- C 41
- D 49

3 Which number is 10 greater than 64?
- A 65
- B 74
- C 605
- D 650

4 Which of these numbers is an odd number?
- A 35
- B 50
- C 92
- D 78

5 What is the missing number in this sequence?
24, 34, 44, 54, 64, 74
- A 45
- B 50
- C 54
- D 55

6 An item costs $1.35. How many cents is that?
- A 5
- B 30
- C 35
- D 135

7 What is the fourth whole number after 27?
- A 23
- B 30
- C 31
- D 274

8 6 + 15 + 5 = ?
- A 26
- B 27
- C 37
- D 80

9 When an odd and an even number are added together, the answer will be
- A even.
- B mostly even.
- C odd.
- D unable to tell.

10 When 21, 8 and 39 are added together, the total is closest to
- A 60.
- B 70
- C 80.
- D 100.

11 What is the missing number in this addition?
26 + ☐18 = 48
- A 12
- B 18
- C 22
- D 74

12 Which number sentence is true?
- A 83 < 78
- B 18 > 61
- C 56 = 65
- D 61 > 57

13 Choose the addition that has the greatest total.
- A 13 + 17
- B 14 + 15
- C 16 + 14
- D 13 + 18

14 Calculate
```
  3 2
+ 6 5
─────
  9 7
```
- A 97
- B 98
- C 107
- D 197

15 Calculate
```
  7 8
- 6 0
─────
  1 8
```
- A 10
- B 18
- C 28
- D 38

16 Calculate
```
  4 3
+ 5 6
─────
  9 9
```
- A 89
- B 99
- C 101
- D 109

17 What is the missing number in this addition?
```
  4 5
  1 ☐
+ 2 3
─────
  7 9
```
- A 0
- B 1
- C 3
- D 8

18 What is the missing number in this subtraction?
```
  5 6
- 3 ☐
─────
  2 1
```
- A 1
- B 3
- C 4
- D 5

19 Joanne had $5. If she spent $1.75, how much does she have left?
- A $3.25
- B $3.75
- C $4.25
- D $4.75

20 What is the least number of coins I need to have $2.75?
- A 4
- B 5
- C 6
- D 7

☞ **Explanations on page 127**

Excel Revise in a Month Year 3 NAPLAN*-style Tests

NUMBER AND ALGEBRA
Whole numbers, addition and subtraction

1 Counting numbers are either **odd** or **even**. Even numbers end with 2, 4, 6, 8 or 0. Odd numbers end with 1, 3, 5, 7 or 9. All even numbers can be exactly divided by 2. Digits are the symbols (0 to 9) we use to write numerals. The numeral 23 508 is made up of five digits.

2 **Factors** are numbers that go evenly into a given number. 1, 2, 3 and 6 are factors of 6.

3 **Zero** has a special place in our number system because it is a place holder. In the number 306, the zero is a place holder for the tens.

4 Our number system is a **base ten system**. It is built up on tens: units, tens (10), ten × ten (100), ten × ten × ten (1000) and so on. Learn to read and write (in numbers and words) the numbers to one thousand.

5 **Expanded notation** is the writing of numerals in an expanded form using the base ten system. It shows the place value of each digit.
Example: 526 = 500 + 20 + 6

6 **Rounding off** allows us to estimate answers. For numbers ending in 1 to 4, **round down** to the lower number. For numbers ending in 5 to 9, **round up** to the higher number.
Examples: 23 rounds down to 20.
47 rounds up to 50.

7 Each digit has a **face** value: for example, 5 (five) represents five units. The value of a digit depends upon its **place** in a numeral. In 847, the 7 has a value of 7 units, the 4 has a value of 4 tens (40), and the 8 has a value of 8 hundreds (800).

8 **Ordinal numbers** are used to order things from first to last (e.g. first, 1st; second, 2nd; third, 3rd). The ordinal number for 20 is 20th.

9 **Signs** you should know include (>) greater than; (<) less than; (=) equals.
Example: 56 > (is greater than) 54.
56 < (is less than) 57.

10 You should know your **doubles** up to 20, then those with totals to 30.

6 + 6 = 12	11 + 11 = 22
7 + 7 = 14	12 + 12 = 24
8 + 8 = 16	13 + 13 = 26
9 + 9 = 18	14 + 14 = 28
10 + 10 = 20	15 + 15 = 30

You should also know how to use the **doubles** shown above in **subtractions**.
Example: 18 − 9 = 9

11 Remember that any simple addition or subtraction can be written **four ways**.
Example: 7 + 8 = 15 or 8 + 7 = 15
or   15 − 7 = 8 or 15 − 8 = 7

12 When two or more numbers are added, we get a **total**: 2 + 3 = 5. The total of 2 and 3 is 5. Another term is **sum**. The sum of 2 and 3 is 5.

13 Additions can be written **horizontally** (21 + 32 = 53) or **vertically**:

```
      2 1
   + 3 2
   ─────
      5 3
```

This addition has two columns: units (ones) and tens. Often the plus sign is left off vertical additions when more than two numbers are being added.

14 When working **vertical additions** with more than one column, start with the right-hand column (units) first, then work to the left (tens, hundreds and so on).

15 Here are some ideas for **adding two-digit numbers**:

Example 1: 32 + 43
Solution: 32 + 43 = 32 + 40 + 3
          = 72 + 3
          = 75

Example 2: 45 + 33
Solution: 45 + 33 = 40 + 30 + 5 + 3
          = 70 + 8
          = 78

Example 3: 25 + 29
Solution: 25 + 29 = 25 + 30 – 1
          = 55 – 1
          = 54

16 Sometimes it can be easier to **pair up numbers first before adding**.

Example: 30 + 16 + 20 + 4
Solution: 30 + 16 + 20 + 4
          = 30 + 20 + 16 + 4
          = 50 + 20
          = 70

17 When a number is subtracted from another number, you get the **difference**.

Example: The difference between 3 and 8 is 5 (8 – 3 = 5).

18 If you have to find a missing number to give a specific total or difference, the best method to use is subtraction.

Example 1: 3 + □ = 8
Solution: 8 – 3 = 5
Example 2: 13 – □ = 8
Solution: 13 – 8 = 5

19 Subtractions can be written **horizontally** (35 – 24 = 11) or **vertically**:

$$\begin{array}{r} 3\,5 \\ -\,2\,4 \\ \hline 1\,1 \end{array}$$

This subtraction has two columns: units (ones) and tens. The minus sign is never left off vertical subtractions.

20 Here are some ideas for **subtracting two-digit numbers**:

Example 1: 45 – 19
Solution: 45 – 19 = 45 – 20 + 1
          = 25 + 1
          = 26

Example 2: 76 – 23
Solution: 76 – 23 = 76 – 20 – 3
          = 56 – 3
          = 53

Example 3: 100 – 57
Solution: 100 – 57 = 100 – 50 – 7
          = 50 – 7
          = 43

21 You need to be able to **use subtraction for solving money problems**. You should know how to give change for amounts of money up to $10.

Example: Tai had $10. She spent $4.50. How much does she have left?

Solution: $10 – $4 = $6.
          Then $6 – 50c = $5.50.

Real Test

NUMBER AND ALGEBRA
Whole numbers, addition and subtraction

20 min

1 Brodie wrote the number three thousand and forty in numerals. What number did he write?

A   3400   B   3004

C   3040   D   34 000

2 John bought a juice which costs $2.30.

JUICE $2.30

How much change did he receive from $3?

A $0.30   B $0.70

C $1.70   D $5.30

3 The expression 2 x 1000 + 4 x 10 + 7 x 1 is to be rewritten.

Write the number in the box: 2047

4 What is the difference between 35 and 14?

A   9   B   19

C   21   D   29

5 What is the sum of 23, 52 and 10?

A   74   B   83

C   85   D   95

6 What number should be written in the box?

A   3   B   4

C   5   D   6

```
2 3  +
3 4
5 7
```

7 Jessa started at 68 and counted forward by 5. What number did she finish at?

A   71   B   72

C   73   D   118

8   34   88   270   29   371   99

What number is the largest even number?

A   88   B   99

C   270   D   371

9 Write 6042 in words.

A   six thousand and forty-two

B   sixty thousand, four hundred and two

C   six thousand, four hundred and two

D   six thousand, four hundred and twenty

10 Four numbers are written on cards:

34   203   136   66

What is the largest number?

A   34   B   203

C   136   D   66

11 Mark had 26 footy cards and gave 11 cards to his brother and 4 to his sister. How many cards did Mark have left?

A   5   B   11

C   12   D   19

12 Subtract 27 from 100. What is the answer?

A   73   B   77

C   83   D   87

13 How many dots are in the display?

A   22   B   24

C   25   D   26

14 Louis is 8 years old and his grandpa is 67 years older than him. How old is Louis' grandpa?

A   59   B   61

C   74   D   75

15

What is the total value of the coins?

A $2.95   B $3.05

C $3.45   D $3.95

16   18   24   17   36   35

Rae noticed that there were two odd numbers in the list of numbers. What is the difference between these two numbers?

A   8   B   18

C   21   D   28

☞ **Answers and explanations on pages 127-128**

NUMBER AND ALGEBRA
Multiplication and division

20 MIN

Circle the correct answer.

MULTIPLICATION

1 $4 + 4 + 4 + 4 + 4 = ?$
A 4 × 4   B 4 + 20
C 5 × 4   D 4 × 4 + 1

2 Abby multiplied a number by 3 and got an answer of 27. What number did she multiply?
A 8   B 9   C 24   D 30

3 There are 12 eggs in one carton. How many eggs in 4 cartons?
A 16   B 24   C 44   D 48

4 What is the missing number in this multiplication?
$5 × \square = 35$
A 5   B 7   C 9   D 30

5 Multiply: 2 1
                  × 3
A 24   B 54   C 54   D 63

6 Billy is tiling a bathroom floor. He has completed two sides. How many tiles will Billy require, in total, to tile the floor?
A 20   B 25
C 30   D 36

7 What is the missing number in this multiplication?
$\$7 × \square = \$28$
A 3   B 4
C 21   D 35

8 $3 × 2 × 0 = ?$
A 0   B 5
C 6   D 7

9 What number is missing?
6, 9, 12, $\square$, 18, 21, 24
A 13   B 14
C 15   D 16

DIVISION

1 $24 ÷ 6 = ?$
A 4   B 6
C 12   D 18

2 Choose the pair of numbers that are factors of 18.
A 4 and 4   B 0 and 17
C 3 and 6   D 10 and 8

3 $7\overline{)42}$
A 6   B 8   C 35   D 49

4 $\dfrac{30}{10} = ?$
A 3   B 15   C 20   D 40

5 Dad shares $24 equally between his three children. How much does each child get?
A $4   B $6
C $8   D $12

6 What is the remainder when 27 is divided by 5?
A 1   B 2   C 3   D 7

7 What is the missing number in this division?
3 2
$3\overline{)9\square}$
A 0   B 1   C 3   D 6

8 $\$30.00 ÷ 6 = ?$
A $5.00   B $5.10
C $24.00   D $50

9 How many times can I take 5 from 45 with zero remaining?
A 8   B 9
C 10   D 40

10 Emily gave half of her cards to Rani. She then gave half of what she had left to her sister. She had 4 cards left. How many cards did Emily start with?
A 8   B 10
C 12   D 16

☞ **Explanations on pages 128-129**

NUMBER AND ALGEBRA
Multiplication and division

MULTIPLICATION

1. **Multiplication** is repeated addition of the same number. The multiplication sign is × and it is sometimes called 'times'. Another term is **lots of** (e.g. 3 lots of 5 equals 15).

2. When two or more numbers are multiplied we get a **product**.
   Example: The product of 3 and 9 is 27.

3. Multiplications can be **written horizontally** (6 × 3 = 18) or vertically:

   $$\begin{array}{r} 2\,1 \\ \times\ \ 4 \\ \hline 8\,4 \end{array}$$

   (the 4 is called the **multiplier**.)
   This multiplication has two columns: units (ones) and tens.

4. Learn your **basic multiplication facts**. This table should help.

×	1	2	3	4	5	6	7	8	9	10
1	1	2	3	4	5	6	7	8	9	10
2	2	4	6	8	10	12	14	16	18	20
3	3	6	9	12	15	18	21	24	27	30
4	4	8	12	16	20	24	28	32	36	40
5	5	10	15	20	25	30	35	40	45	50
6	6	12	18	24	30	36	42	48	54	60
7	7	14	21	28	35	42	49	56	63	70
8	8	16	24	32	40	48	56	64	72	80
9	9	18	27	36	45	54	63	72	81	90
10	10	20	30	40	50	60	70	80	90	100

   To use the table you read across and down.
   Example: 6 × 5 = 30
   (follow the grey boxes)

5. When working **vertical multiplications** with **more than one column**, start with the right-hand column (units) and then work to the left (tens, hundreds and so on).

6. Make sure you can see the **relationship between multiplied numbers**: 3 × 4 = 12, so 4 × 3 = 12.

7. Multiplication may also be written in **reverse form**.
   Example: 12 = 3 × 4 or 12 = 4 × 3

8. The same rules for **carrying** apply to multiplication as for addition.

9. When **zero** is multiplied by any number the product is always **zero**.
   Examples: 5 × 0 = 0, and
   3 × 3 × 2 × 0 = 0

10. Learn to count in **groups** of all numbers up to 10 so that you can find the missing numbers in sequences.
    Example: 3, 6, 9, 12 and so on;
    5, 10, 15, 20, 25 and so on.

11. A shortcut to use when you are **multiplying by 10** is to add a zero to the whole number being multiplied.
    Example: 10 × 37 = 370, and
    10 × 59 = 590

12. When **estimating** a product, round off the number first.
    Example: Estimate 41 × 19
    Solution: As 40 × 20 = 800, an estimate for 41 × 19 is 800.

DIVISION

1. **Division** is repeated subtraction of the same number. The division sign is ÷ . Another term is **share** (e.g. share $6 equally between 3 girls).

2. When one number is divided by another number we get a **quotient**.
   Example: The quotient when 8 is divided by 2 is 4.

3. Division can be **written in several ways**:

   24 ÷ 6 or $6\overline{)24}$ or $6\underline{)24}$ or $\dfrac{24}{6}$

4. Use the **multiplication table** to learn basic division facts.

   7 × 8 = 56 → 56 ÷ 8 = 7 and 56 ÷ 7 = 8

5 **Remainders** are the numbers left over when a number cannot be divided evenly. The remainder cannot be the same size or larger than the number you are dividing by.

Example: When 7 is divided by 4, the remainder is 3. This is written as '1 r 3'.

6 If a number is divisible by another, then the remainder is zero and the second number is a **factor** of the first.

Example: The factors of 12 are 1, 2, 3, 4, 6 and 12.

7 There are **several methods** of working a **division problem**.

a Using repeated subtraction:

$37 \div 11 = (37 - 11 - 11 - 11 = 4)$
  $= 3$ (elevens) r 4

b Using knowledge of basic multiplication facts, start with the left-hand side (hundreds) then work to the right (tens, units):

$$\begin{array}{r} 301 \\ 3\overline{)903} \end{array}$$

(3 into 9 = 3, 3 into 0 = 0 and 3 into 3 = 1.)

8 When **dividing (sharing) money**, don't be too concerned about the cent point. Divide the amount to be divided as if the cent point has no value BUT add it in directly above the cent point in the operation or two places to the left from the right-hand end.

$$\begin{array}{r} \$4.50 \\ 4\overline{)\$18.00} \end{array}$$

9 When **zero is divided by any number**, the quotient (answer) is always zero:

$0 \div 14 = 0$ *or* $14\overline{)0}^{\,0}$

Real Test

NUMBER AND ALGEBRA
Multiplication and division

20 MIN

1 Jason added half of twenty to double nine. What is Jason's answer?
  A 10
  B 18
  C 19
  D 28

2 A dog has 4 legs and a chicken has 2 legs. On a farm there are 3 dogs and 5 chickens. How many legs do the animals have?
  A 8
  B 14
  C 18
  D 22

3

CHOCOLATE   80c

Elene bought 3 chocolate bars. What will her total cost be?
  A 83 cents
  B $2.40
  C $3.20
  D $3.50

4 Which of these has a remainder of 3?
  A 13 divided by 5
  B 12 divided by 4
  C 17 divided by 4
  D 16 divided by 5

5 Kiwi fruit is on sale at 3 for 60 cents. What is the greatest number of kiwi fruit that can be purchased for $3.00?
  A 5
  B 9
  C 15
  D 18

6 What is the best estimate of 29 × 47?
  A 20 × 40
  B 20 × 50
  C 30 × 50
  D 30 × 40

7 403 is multiplied by 10. What is the answer?
  A 43
  B 413
  C 430
  D 4030

8 The dots are to be arranged into groups of six. How many dots will be left over?

  A 1
  B 2
  C 3
  D 4

9 There are 6 vases with 5 flowers in each vase. How many flowers are there altogether?
  A 9
  B 20
  C 24
  D 30

10 Jocelyn plans to give 4 stickers to each of her 5 friends. How many stickers has she altogether?
  A 1
  B 16
  C 18
  D 20

11 Write a number in the box to make the number sentence correct:

  6 × [9] = 54

12 While Michael is travelling to school he notices that his train stops for 3 minutes at each of 7 stations. What is the total amount of time that the train is stopped at the stations?
  A 4 minutes
  B 10 minutes
  C 16 minutes
  D 21 minutes

13 At his party Max has 3 pizzas and each pizza is to be cut into 8 slices. If 15 slices are eaten, how many slices of pizza are left over?
  A 9
  B 11
  C 15
  D 24

14 In her wallet Mim has three 50 cent coins and two 20 cent coins. How much money does Mim have altogether?
  A 54 cents
  B 70 cents
  C $1.70
  D $1.90

15 Jack gave his three nephews an equal share of $66. How much will each of the nephews receive?
  A $11
  B $22
  C $33
  D $63

16 Tiffany bought 2 pencils and an eraser.

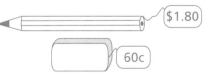

$1.80

60c

How much change did she get from $5?
  A 60 cents
  B 70 cents
  C 80 cents
  D $4.20

☞ **Answers and explanations on page 129**

SPELLING
Making plurals from nouns

- With most spelling rules there are exceptions. This is because English words come from many different languages (e.g. 'café' comes from French and 'pasta' comes from Italian).
- You should know the alphabet and the difference between the vowels (a, e, i, o, u) and consonants (all the other letters).

Key Points

1 With most words, to make a plural you simply add an 's'.
Examples: cats, days, taxis, tigers, hares, clams

2 To make plurals with words that end with a consonant + 'y', change the 'y' to 'i' and add 'es'.
Examples: cry → cries, jelly → jellies, fairy → fairies, city → cities, puppy → puppies

3 To make plurals of words that end with 's', 'ss', 'x', 'zz', 'ch' and 'sh', add 'es'.
Examples: bus → buses, class → classes, fox → foxes, buzz → buzzes, branch → branches, bush → bushes

4 For some words ending in 'f' or 'fe', change the 'f' to a 'v' and add 's'.
Examples: wife → wives, elf → elves, hoof → hooves

5 For some words that end with a single 'o', add 'es'.
Examples: potato → potatoes, tomato → tomatoes, volcano → volcanoes
Note that there are quite a few common exceptions to this rule, such as radios and solos.

6 A few plurals have unusual spellings. You will just have to learn them!
Examples: child → children, tooth → teeth, man → men, woman → women, goose → geese, mouse → mice

7 A few words refer simply to a substance's mass. *Examples:* water, rice, flour

8 There are a few common words that don't change at all. *Examples:* deer, fish, sheep, tuna

Test Your Skills

Learn the words below. A common method of learning and self-testing is the **LOOK, SAY, COVER, WRITE, CHECK** method. If you make any mistakes, you should rewrite the word three times correctly, immediately. This is so you will become familiar with the correct spelling. If the word is especially difficult, rewrite it several more times or keep a list of words that you can check regularly.

This week's theme words: DAD'S SHED

tool	_____	nail	_____
tools	_____	nails	_____
bench	_____	zero	_____
benches	_____	zeroes	_____
knife	_____	lorry	_____
knives	_____	lorries	_____
box	_____	pliers	_____
boxes	_____	hammer	_____

Write any troublesome words three times: _____ _____

_____ _____

Real Test

1 The spelling mistakes in these sentences have been highlighted.
Write the correct spelling for each highlighted word in the box.

a   Dad has two glases on the work bench.

glasses ✓

b   Make sure you are erly for your lesson!

early ✓

c   The skrews to fix the door are rusty.

screws ✓

d   You will have to scroub your dirty hands!

~~scrotbry~~ scrub ✓

e   How meny people are going on the camp?

many ✓

f   The dog sleeped for an hour after his run.

~~slepe~~ slept ✓

g   Peg was fileing her nails while watching TV.

Filing ✓

h   The teacher sed my work was excellent.

Said ✓

2 The spelling mistakes in these labels have been highlighted. Write the correct spelling for each highlighted word in the box.

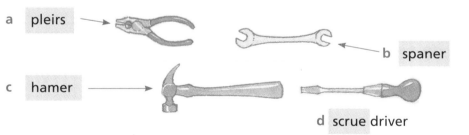

a   pleirs

b   spaner

c   hamer

d   scrue driver

pliers ✓

Spanner ✓

hammer ✓

Screw ✓

3 Read the text *Fat Freddy*.
Each line has a word that is incorrect. Write the correct spelling of the word in the box.

Fat Freddy

a   Freddy was geting so fat he could not

getting ✓

b   do up his belt or tie his shoo laces.

Shoe ✓

c   His feet where now so hard to reach.

were ✓

d   He tired sitting down and lifting his foot but

Tried ✓

e   all that happened was his leg jest stuck

Just ✓

f   straight out in front of his fat boddy.

body ✓

☞ **Answers on page 130**

GRAMMAR AND PUNCTUATION
Types of sentences and articles

Key Points

1 All sentences start with **capital letters**. There are four main types of sentences.

a **Statements** end with a full stop. A simple statement contains one verb (an action word) and makes sense on its own.
Example: The frog <u>jumped</u> into the pond.
More **complex statements** can contain two or more verbs and two or more ideas.
Example: The frog <u>jumped</u> into the pond when the boys <u>climbed</u> onto the rocks.

b **Questions** end with a question mark. Questions usually need answers.
Example: What <u>are</u> you doing? (Answer: I am getting a drink.)

c **Exclamations** end with an exclamation mark. Exclamation sentences are often quite short.
Example: <u>Grab</u> the rope!

d **Commands** end with a full stop (or an exclamation mark if they are particularly sharp).
Example: Finish your homework in your room.

2 The small words 'a', 'an' and 'the' are called **articles**.

a We use the word '**the**' before special objects or people.
Examples: Dad put his hat on <u>the hook</u> by the door. (This means that Dad put his hat on one special hook, not just any old hook.)
<u>The school bus</u> is always on time. (The writer is referring to one special bus—the school bus—not just any school bus.)

b The word '**a**' is used when you are talking or writing about objects in general.
Examples: <u>A bus</u> should come along soon. (The writer is not referring to any particular bus—just any bus that will come along soon. The writer doesn't know which one will come.)
Dad put his hat on <u>a hook</u> by the door. (We are not told if it was a particular hook.)

c The word '**an**' is used before words that start with vowels: <u>an</u> umbrella, <u>an</u> ice block, <u>an</u> orange. It is also used with a silent 'h': <u>an</u> hour, <u>an</u> honour.
Example: Erin took <u>an</u> apple from the fruit bowl. (The writer means that Erin took no particular apple from the bowl, she just took one of them.)

Test Your Skills

1 Put the correct punctuation marker in brackets at the end of these sentences.
a Sally and Margo are friends ( )
b Did Ms Wong give you the change ( )
c Stop, wait ( )
d Whatever you buy, don't tell Mum ( )
e Will Sam come swimming today ( )

2 Write 'a', 'an' or 'the' in the spaces.
It had been _____ dry summer but Sandy still wanted to join _____ Scouts on __ excursion. One was planned for _____ Booti National Park. He had bought _____ new backpack for _____ trip. He already had _____ small safety first kit, _____ compass, _____ air mattress _____ waterproof watch and _____ most important item of all — _____ old hat. Each Scout would be given _____ water bottle.

GRAMMAR AND PUNCTUATION
Types of sentences and articles

15 min

1 Which of the following correctly completes this sentence?
Tim and Tom _____ in my class at school.

is	are	am	was
A	B	C	D

2 Which of the following correctly completes this sentence?
A bee is _____ insect that lives in a hive.

a	the	an	what
A	B	C	D

3 Which of the following correctly completes this sentence?
Molly is _____ only person who can keep score.

a	the	and	an
A	B	C	D

4 Which of the following correctly completes this sentence?
Our cat climbed _____ the fence and into the neighbour's back yard.

over	on	above	long
A	B	C	D

5 Which of the following correctly completes this sentence?
Neither Spot _____ Rover will chase cars.

or	either	and	nor
A	B	C	D

6 Which sentence has the correct punctuation?
A   The Premier of Queensland toured the outback.
B   The Premier of Queensland toured the Outback.
C   The premier of Queensland toured the outback.
D   The premier of Queensland toured the Outback.

Read the text *My Pony*. The text has some gaps. Choose the best option to fill each gap.

My Pony
We have a block of land in the bush.

We _____ a horse on our land. His name

is Silver. _____ is plenty of grass near

the gate _____ lots of shady trees

7
keep	kept	keeped	keept
A	B	C	D

8
there	Where	There	Their
A	B	C	D

9
and	an	or	but
A	B	C	D

☞ **Answers and explantions on page 130**

Real Test

GRAMMAR AND PUNCTUATION
Types of sentences and articles

_____ the creek near the back fence.

10   up   along   in   above

     Ⓐ   B   C   D

I like to ride Silver early in _____ morning

11   a   an   the   this

     A   B   C   D

before it gets hot. What do you think _____

12   !   .   ,   ?

     A   B   C   D

13   Which sentence has the correct punctuation?
     A   Has Tony finished his meal!
     B   Has Tony finished his meal
     C   Has Tony finished his meal.
     D   Has Tony finished his meal?

14   Which sentence has the correct punctuation?
     A   I saw Harleys bike under trees near the bus stop.
     B   I saw Harley's bike under trees near the bus stop.
     C   I saw Harley's bike under tree's near the bu's stop.
     D   I saw Harleys bike under tree's near the bus stop.

15   Which of the following correctly completes this sentence?
     The rains came just as we _____ the shed.
        left   lefted   leaved   leaf
        A   B   C   D

16   Which of the following correctly completes the sentence?
     The new bike can go _____ than my old bike.
       more fast   fast   faster   fastest
        A   B   C   D

17   Circle a letter to show where the missing full stop (.) should go.
     Dennis can carry the paper ↟ and ↟ Lindy will carry the mail ↟ and new CD ↟
               Ⓐ   Ⓑ   Ⓒ   Ⓓ

18   Choose the word that is not required in this sentence.
     A circular ring was drawn around the wrong answer.
       circular   drawn   around   wrong
        A   B   C   D

☞ **Answers and explanations on page 130**

A **narrative** is a type of writing that tells a story. Its main purpose is to entertain us.

Writers of narratives create experiences that are shared with the reader. To do this, they use **techniques** such as figurative language (similes and metaphors), different types of sentences, different sentence lengths, direct speech and different paragraph lengths.

In many narratives, the **author** is the person who wrote the story. The **narrator** is the person (referred to as 'I') in the story who tells the story.

Read this extract from *The Heron and the Crab*, an Indian folk tale, and answer the questions. Circle the correct answer.

There was once a shaded pond, far away from the fields and villages in India. Many fish lived in the pond. Each day a heron stood in the pond and caught any foolish fish that swam too close. He would snatch a fish in his beak then wade ashore to eat it. The fish knew the heron was their enemy. As the heron got older he got slower and even foolish fish could escape his beak. This worried the heron. He could die of hunger if he did not catch fish. He needed a secret plan.

Over the next few days the animals noticed that the heron did not try to catch any fish. This was strange behaviour for a heron. And he had a sad look in his eyes. A crab who lived in the pond asked the heron, 'Why aren't you catching fish? Why are you so sad?'

The heron sighed sadly, 'This pond has been our home for many years. But just a few days ago I heard bad news. It will make everyone in the pond sad.'

'We are happy in our pond. This has been our home for many years. What can make us sad?' asked the crab.

The heron hung his head. 'Some villagers know the pond is full of fish and are coming with nets,' he lied.

'That is bad news. When are they coming?' asked the crab.

'Maybe in a few days,' shrugged the heron.

While they were talking some fish came by to listen. They became very frightened and confused. They said to the heron, 'What should we do? We don't want to be trapped in nets to be eaten by villagers.'

---

① This extract is most likely from

    A a true adventure.   **B** a mystery novel.   **C** a fable.   **D** a legend.

② Which word has a similar meaning to the word 'snatch'?

    A grab   **B** snap   **C** trap   **D** hold

③ Which word best describes the heron's behaviour?

    A helpful   **B** confused   **C** sneaky   **D** friendly

④ In the extract, which statement is true?

    A The villagers were about to net the pond.   **B** The crab was trying to catch the fish.

    C The fish knew the heron was a friend.   **D** The heron was pretending to be worried.

⑤ When did the heron say the villagers were going to start netting the pond?

    A when he got old   **B** in a few days   **C** not for many years   **D** immediately

⑥ Who should the fish be most afraid of?

    A the villagers   **B** the heron   **C** fishermen   **D** the crab

Answers: 1 C 2 A 3 C 4 D 5 B 6 B

☞ Explanations on pages 130-131

Real Test

READING
Understanding narratives

Read this extract from *Simon's Solution* by Alan Horsfield and answer the questions. Circle the correct answer.

Simon saw his father look grimly towards the sky. Simon's father was not a grim man but he didn't like what he saw. When Simon looked up he saw that sky was full of black, noisy birds. Some were making big, lazy circles over the fields. Others were darting all over the place, flapping their wings impatiently. Simon's father waved his fist angrily at them. 'Beat it!' he yelled.

Then he turned to Simon. 'Lots of birds up there,' he complained, shaking his head with annoyance. 'That's not good.'

His father was sitting on the seat of his old red tractor looking over his corn crop. After the recent rain it was almost ready to harvest.

Simon was squatting on the trailer. It was school holidays and Simon had been helping his father mend a fence down by the creek. 'Dad,' said Simon, 'won't those birds eat our corn?'

'What do you think we should do?' asked Simon's father, rubbing his whiskery chin. 'Can't spend all day shaking my fist at them and shouting at them. I'm off to town later, anyway.'

'Hey, we need a scarecrow!' declared Simon. 'To scare the crows!'

'Might work,' agreed his father. 'Could you make one?'

Simon thought for a moment. He'd seen pictures of scarecrows in books. It shouldn't be too difficult. 'I made a bookcase for Mum once. It shouldn't be too hard,' said Simon. 'We have lots of bits and pieces in the shed.'

'Then you've got yourself a job!' called Simon's father as he put the tractor into gear and headed back to the farmhouse. 'Hang on!'

1 Where were Simon and his father?
   A   in a shed   B   on a farm   C   in a town   D   at a school

2 What does the word 'grim' mean?
   A   dirty   B   annoyed   C   harsh   D   impatient

3 Where was Simon going to get the pieces for his scarecrow?
   A   in town   B   in the corn field C   in the shed   D   from his mother

4 What had Simon been doing with his father?
   A   fixing a fence   B   making a scarecrow
   C   planting corn   D   chasing crows

5 Simon was not at school because he
   A   lived out of town.   B   was helping his father.
   C   was on holidays.   D   was making a bookcase.

6 Which word best describes how Simon felt when he was told he could make a scarecrow?
   A   excited   B   annoyed   C   worried   D   upset

7 Which statement about Simon is correct?
   A   Simon was driving the tractor.   B   Simon was about to help his mother.
   C   Simon was helping scare the birds.   D   Simon had once made a bookcase.

☞ **Answers and explanations on page 131**

Real Test

READING
Understanding narratives

Read the extract from *Fearless Brian* by Alan Horsfield and answer the questions.

Brian was lying on his bed staring at the ceiling when his mother called, 'Brian, have you done your homework?'

'No,' he called back, 'I was just saving a dolphin from a school of hungry sharks. My air tank is almost empty!'

Brian, the daydreamer. He spent hours daydreaming about how brave he was with wild animals. He could daydream anywhere, anytime, even in front of TV. 'Brian. Homework!'

Now his father was getting cross.

'Dad, I have to get the dolphin into safe water before I can do any homework.'

'Just make it snappy! Dinner will be in ten minutes!' his mother warned.

What's wrong with a little daydreaming, he thought. After all, his name, Brian, did mean 'strong and powerful'.

It was the same the next day. He was sitting at his desk not doing homework, just daydreaming.

His baby sister, Devona, was sitting on the floor watching him. He didn't even know she was there! That's because Brian was a lion tamer in a circus. He was alone, in a cage, with three huge lions.

All the lights were shining on him. All was quiet. The audience could hear the lions' tails swish as the lions watched Brian. People were afraid Brian would be eaten. But Brian was not afraid. He was strong and powerful.

Brian took a small chair and walked towards the biggest lion.

Devona giggled.

1 What was Brian doing in his bedroom?
- A   saving dolphins
- B   filling an airtank
- C   his homework
- D   daydreaming

2 In the extract, how many people are there in Brian's family?
- A   two
- B   three
- C   four
- D   five

3 What word could best describe Brian's mother's feelings about his daydreaming?
- A   excited
- B   frustrated
- C   delighted
- D   afraid

4 What is Brian most likely to use the small chair for?
- A   safety and defence
- B   to sit on
- C   to annoy the lion
- D   to climb onto

5 Why did Brian think that he was brave?
- A   that's what his name meant
- B   he could protect dolphins from sharks
- C   his mother let him do dangerous things
- D   people were amazed by his daring

6 Write the numbers 1, 2, 3 and 4 in the boxes to show the order in which they happened.
- 2   Brian daydreamed about the circus.
- 4   Devona giggled.
- 1   Brian daydreamed about a shark attack.
- 3   Brian's mother called him for a meal.

7 What sound is a 'swish' sound most like?
- A   a swarm of flies
- B   a light breeze
- C   a gushing stream
- D   sausages sizzling

☞ **Answers and explanations on pages 131-132**

Read this extract from *Fancy Dress Party* by Alan Horsfield and answer the questions.

On Tuesday I found a letter in our letterbox. To my surprise it was an invitation for me.

I loved fancy dress parties and Amanda always had the best prizes. I showed the invitation to Mum and Dad.
'That looks like fun, Tim,' said Dad. 'What do you know that's red?'
Suddenly I couldn't think of anything.
Mum said, 'How about a fire engine? Or the Little Red Engine?'
Dad laughed. 'A red robin?'
I didn't like any of those ideas. They wouldn't win a prize!
Then we had lots of ideas. A red balloon. A red rose—or a red nose. A red-headed boy.
None of those ideas would win a prize.
'If you were a girl you could go as Little Red Riding Hood,' laughed Mum.
'What about a red chilli pepper?' joked Dad.
'A red apple?' suggested Mum.
We had run out of ideas. Mum said, 'Let's have a rest and try again tomorrow.' Tomorrow was Wednesday.
Wednesday was no better. We came up with a red-hot poker, a red Martian and even a red tomato! Our ideas were getting worse and Saturday was getting closer. There was no way I could get a prize as a red tomato.
On Thursday we were almost out of red ideas. Mum suggested a red tomato sauce bottle.
Dad said, 'Red ants?' He was out of ideas too.

1 Tim liked going to Amanda's parties because of the
   A food. B prizes. C games. D costumes.

2 What is the most likely reason Amanda decided to have a 'red' party?
   A it was her favourite colour B her name had the word 'red' in it
   C she had red hair D everybody can easily get a red costume

3 Who thought of the idea of going to the party as a red robin?
   A Amanda B Mum C Dad D Tim

4 What was Tim most likely feeling by Thursday?
   A worried B excited C puzzled D confused

5 For Amanda, the word 'summoned' is a fun way to say
   A called. B invited. C ordered. D begged.

6 How did Tim get his party invitation?
   A it was slipped under the door B by telephone
   C it was handed to him D by mail ☞ **Answers and explanations on page 132**

READING
Understanding narratives

Read the extract from *Puppets* by Carole Hooper and answer the questions.

Javanese* shadow puppets

The Javanese wayang kulit are shadow puppets made from goat or buffalo skin which has been oiled or coloured. These flat puppets are of various sizes and range in height from 40 to 150 centimetres. They are carefully cut out and painted.

The puppets are held against a screen on rods made from strips of horn, and are moved by the puppeteer, called the dalang. A light shines on the puppets, making them appear as shadows on the other side of the screen. The dalang makes up the dialogue for the puppets and also directs the gamalan orchestra which sits behind him and plays music during the performance.

Wayang kulit puppet shows are performed frequently and often last all night. The stories performed by the puppets are usually of a religious nature, such as the Hindu stories of the Ramayana or Mahabbarata, which show the battle between the forces of good and evil.

*Note: Java is in Indonesia.

1 This information would most likely be found in a
  A novel.
  C manual
  B travel book.
  D sports magazine.

2 What is the meaning of *frequently* in this text?
  A very slowly
  C over and over again
  B with great care
  D over long periods of time

3 The man who makes the puppets move and talk also has another task. What is that task? Write your answer on the line.
To conduct the orchestra.

4 The Javanese puppets are made from
  A plastic.
  C cloth.
  B wood.
  D animal hide.

5 What is a dalang?
  A a man who moves a puppet
  C music played during a play
  B a story for a Javanese puppet play
  D material used to make puppets

6 What are the rods that move the puppets made from?
  A wood
  B bone
  C metal
  D horn

7 Which statement is true? Javanese puppet plays
  A are shadow plays on screens.
  C require several puppeteers.
  B do not have speaking parts.
  D use puppets on strings.

☞ **Answers and explanations on page 132**

GENERAL WRITING TIPS

Each weekly writing plan provides either two or three exercises. This allows for two forty-minute writing sessions each week, with any extra exercises to be used for practice at a later time.

Writing Tests are designed to test your ability to express ideas, feelings and points of view. You will be assessed on:

- the thought and content of your writing
- the structure and organisation of your ideas
- the expression, style and appropriate use of language of your writing
- the amount you write in the given time.

To get the best results, follow these steps.

Step 1 – Before you start writing

- **Read the question**. Do you understand the type of writing you are being asked to do? If the question wants you to write an explanation, you should write an explanation—not a story or any other type of writing. Read the instructions carefully. Ask yourself if you should be describing, explaining, entertaining, telling a story, expressing a point of view, expressing an emotion or persuading the reader.
- **Check the stimulus material carefully**. *Stimulus material* means the topic, title, picture, words, phrases or extract of writing you are given to base your writing on. Your writing must be based on this material.
- **What writing style?** If you are given a choice of writing styles (text types), pick the style you are most comfortable with.
- **Warning**: don't try to make a pre-planned piece of writing (that is, something you have already written) fit the stimulus material you are given.

Step 2 – Jot down points

Give yourself a few minutes before you start to get your thoughts in order and jot down points. You won't have time to write a draft. Depending on the writing style required, jot down points on:

- who (characters), why (reasons for action), where (setting), when (time)
- sequences of events/arguments/points
- any good ideas you suddenly have
- how to include the senses and your feelings.

Remember: you can choose not to use any ideas that don't fit into your final approach.

Step 3 – Make a brief outline

List the points or events in order. This will become your framework. It can be changed as you write.

GENERAL WRITING TIPS

Step 4 – Start writing

- Make your **paragraphing** work for you. New paragraphs are usually needed for
  - new incidents in stories
  - changes in time or place
  - descriptions that move from one sense to another (e.g. from sight to sound)
  - a change in the character using direct speech.
- Don't forget that your **vocabulary** is being tested. Don't use unusual words or big words just to impress the assessor. A mistake here will show that you might not understand the words properly.
- It is important that you **complete your piece of writing**. Unfinished work may lose you marks, as will extremely short pieces of writing.
- Get as much of the **punctuation, spelling and grammar** right as you can, but allow yourself a couple of minutes after you finish to proofread your work. You won't have time to go over it in detail, but a quick check at the end will help.
- If you are writing a story, know the **ending** before you start. Try to make the ending unusual and well-written—not just *I woke up and found it was only a dream!*
- If you are asked to give a **point of view**, think through the evidence you can use to support your 'argument' so that you can build to a strong conclusion.
- If you are including **descriptions** in your writing, think about all the senses—sights, smells, tastes, sounds and physical feelings. You may also include an **emotional response**.
- Have a **concluding sentence** that 'rounds off' your work.
- Keep your **handwriting** reasonably neat (i.e. readable).

Step 5 – When you finish

When you finish, **re-read** your work and do a quick check for spelling, punctuation, capital letters and grammar.

Check the Writing section (www.nap.edu.au/naplan/about-each-domain/writing/writing.html) **of the official NAPLAN website for up-to-date and important information on the Writing Test.** From 2008 to 2010 students were required to write a narrative text and from 2011 to 2013 a persuasive text was required. In 2013 teachers, parents and students were advised that the 2014 Writing Test would be either persuasive OR narrative. The 2014 and 2015 Writing Tests were persuasive. The type of text for 2016 will again be either persuasive OR narrative so students should prepare for both. You can also find marking guidelines on the NAPLAN website that outline the criteria markers use when assessing your writing. Sample Writing Tests are also provided.

TIPS FOR WRITING PERSUASIVE TEXTS

Persuasive texts (expositions or opinions) are used to 'argue' the case for or against a particular action, plan or point of view—to *persuade* others to see it your way. Persuasive texts need to be well organised and clear so that readers will understand and be convinced of your arguments.

When writing persuasive texts it is best to keep the following points in mind. They will help you get the best possible mark.

Before you start writing

■ Read the question carefully. You will probably be asked to write your reaction to a particular question or statement, such as *Dogs should be kept out of parks*. Most of the topics that you will be asked to comment on are very general. This means you will probably be writing about something you know and can draw upon your experience. When writing your personal opinion you may include such phrases as *I think, I believe* and *It is important*. Remember to sound confident. Some common ways for the question to be worded are: *Give your opinion on ...; Do you agree or disagree?; What do you think is/are ... ?; What changes would you like to see ... ?; Is ... a good idea or a bad idea?*

■ You will be expected to give your reasons. Sometimes the question may actually state *Give your reasons*. Remember: the stance taken in a persuasive text is not wrong, as long as the writer has evidence to support his or her opinion. How the opinion is supported is as important as the opinion itself.

■ Give yourself a few minutes before you start writing to get your thoughts in order and jot down points.

The introduction

■ Right from the beginning it is important to let the reader know what position you have taken or what you believe. You can do this via the title or in the first line or paragraph, which may include a brief preview of the main arguments and some background information.

The body

■ **Follow the structure of persuasive texts.** As persuasive texts aim to convince readers, your reasons must be logical and easily understood. You must provide both arguments (points) and evidence to support the arguments.

■ **Correctly paragraph your writing.** Use paragraphs with topic sentences to organise your information. Without paragraphs your arguments become confused and difficult to follow. Use one paragraph for each idea or argument. Arguments can be ordered according to your choice. They can be 'numbered', e.g. *firstly, secondly, finally*.

■ **Make sure your arguments (or points) are relevant.** They must add to your case. 'Waffle' and unnecessary detail don't improve a persuasive text. It is better to stick to the facts without getting sidetracked. Once you have made a point there is no need to repeat it.

■ **Use interesting, precise words.** Include strong persuasive words such as *must, believe, important* or *certainly*. Avoid common words that carry little or no meaning, such as *good*. You can state your arguments using sentences beginning with words such as *firstly, furthermore* or *finally*.

■ **Vary the types and lengths of sentences and the words that begin each sentence.** If your writing includes a personal opinion, try to avoid too many sentences starting with *I*.

■ **Use impersonal writing**, although personal opinions can be part of the text.

The conclusion

■ The final paragraph must restate your position more forcefully and wrap up your case. It can include a recommendation.

When you have finished writing give yourself a few moments to read through your persuasive text. Quickly check spelling and punctuation and insert any words that have been accidentally left out. Direct speech is not a feature of persuasive texts. Indirect speech (reported speech) does not have speech marks (" ").

You will find a sample annotated persuasive text on the following page. The question is from Sample Test 1 on page 92. Read the persuasive text and notes before you begin your first Writing Test. This piece of writing has been analysed based on the marking criteria used by markers to assess the NAPLAN Writing Test.
Remember: this sample was not written under exam conditions.

Vocabulary

- A good variety of precise **verb** types are used to establish strong, informed arguments.
- **Nouns** are used to make generalised statements.
- **Adverbs** and **adjectives** are well selected to qualify statements.
- The pronoun *I* is used sparingly.

Sentence structure

- A good variety of sentence beginnings (e.g. *Having, Tissues*) are used.
- A variety of sentence types and lengths are used.
- Topic sentences are used to introduce each paragraph's main idea.
- Exclamations are used to good effect.

Ideas

- Ideas are well balanced to create a sense of rational, logical argument.
- A strong viewpoint is expressed through careful choice of words.
- Ideas are presented positively and forcefully.

Punctuation

- Punctuation, including apostrophes and full stops, is correctly applied.

Spelling

- There are no spelling mistakes of common or unusual words.

Structure

Year 3 Sample Persuasive Writing
(a sample answer to the question on page 92)

A box of tissues should be supplied for each Year 3 student's desk.

I believe it would be a good idea if schools supplied tissues for students. The best way to do this is to have a box on each desk. Tissues are better than the old-fashioned hankie some children bring to school.

First of all, tissues are disposable. Hankies are kept in pockets often for days after they have been used. Germs are not destroyed, and breed in the warm pockets. Sometimes used hankies are kept in school bags with books and even lunch boxes. This is a perfect way to spread germs. Hankies are a health hazard!

Tissues are used once and then put in a waste bin. Every class has a rubbish bin. Germs are kept away from all students. Bins are emptied daily by cleaners wearing protective gloves.

Having a box of tissues on each desk means that students who need a tissue in a hurry don't have to rush to get one from the teacher's desk. This disturbs nearby students and interrupts the teacher when she is helping individual students.

Tissues on desks provide a quick way to clean up any mess on that desk. If water is spilt then it's a simple matter to wipe it up without a fuss.

Finally hankies have to be washed. Washing hankies means wasting water when it can be avoided. Washing wastes valuable time for parents who want quality time with their children.

I support the idea of supplying a box of tissues for each Year 3 desk. There are health benefits. It is also a convenient way to provide tissues. Tissues are the modern way to deal with coughs and colds. No-one really wants dirty old hankies. It is time schools kept up with changing conditions.

Audience

- The audience is readily identified (Year 3 students).
- Readers are quickly engaged in a relevant issue.
- A brief statement outlines the issue to be discussed.
- Background information is provided to give context to the points raised.

Persuasive techniques

- Arguments are organised into separate paragraphs.
- Points raised are obviously important to the writer in a personal way.
- Evidence and examples are used to support the argument.
- Objectivity is maintained throughout the writing.

Text structure

- The text contains a well-organised introduction, body and conclusion.
- The writer refers regularly to words used in the topic.

Paragraphing

- New paragraphs are used for new arguments and the summary.

Cohesion

- The final paragraph establishes where the writer stands on the issue.
- The concluding sentence is forceful and personal.

Real Test and Tips

WRITING
Persuasive text 1

40 MIN

Before you start, read the General writing tips on pages 20–21 and the Tips for writing persuasive texts on page 22.

Today you are going to write a persuasive text, often called an exposition. The purpose of writing a persuasive text is to influence or change a reader's thoughts or opinions on a particular topic or subject. Your aim is to convince a reader that your opinion is sensible and logical. Successful persuasive writing is always well planned. Persuasive texts may include advertisements, letters to newspapers, speeches and newspaper editorials, as well as arguments in debates.

Students should be allowed to celebrate their birthdays in class.

What do you think about this topic? Do you support or reject this idea? Write to convince a reader of your opinions.

Before you start writing, give some thought to:
- whether you strongly agree or strongly disagree with this plan   *once / year*
- reasons or evidence for your arguments   *birthday only comes makes you feel happy, excited, special you get attention*
- a brief but definite conclusion—list some of your main points and add a personal opinion
- the structure of a persuasive text, which begins with a well-organised introduction, followed by a body of arguments or points, and finally a conclusion that restates the writer's position.

Don't forget to:
- plan your writing before you start—make a list of important points you wish to make
- write in correctly formed sentences and take care with paragraphing
- choose your words carefully, and pay attention to your spelling and punctuation
- write neatly but don't waste time
- quickly check your persuasive text once you have finished—your position must be clear to the reader.

Remember: the stance taken in a persuasive text is not wrong, as long as the writer has evidence to support his or her opinion. How the opinion is supported is as important as the opinion itself.

Start writing here.

I believe students should celebrate their birthdays in class because birthday only come once a year and you are celebrated as an individual. It makes you happy and feel special. Our friends celebrate you in class is good because all of your class can be there but at a party not every one is there. I support the idea because all of your friends are there to make you feel happy and special.

☞ **Marking guide on pages 132-133**

Real Test and Tips

40 min

Before you start, read the General writing tips on pages 20–21 and the Tips for writing persuasive texts on page 22.

Today you are going to write a persuasive text, often called an exposition. The purpose of writing a persuasive text is to influence or change a reader's thoughts or opinions on a particular topic or subject. Your aim is to convince a reader that your opinion is sensible and logical. Successful persuasive writing is always well planned. Persuasive texts may include advertisements, letters to newspapers, speeches and newspaper editorials, as well as arguments in debates.

Some students think Music is a more important subject than Science.

What do you think about this idea? Do you agree or disagree with this opinion? Write to convince a reader of your opinion.

Before you start writing, give some thought to:
- whether you strongly agree or strongly disagree with this plan
- reasons or evidence for your arguments
- a brief but definite conclusion—list some of your main points and add a personal opinion
- the structure of a persuasive text, which begins with a well-organised introduction, followed by a body of arguments or points, and finally a conclusion that restates the writer's position.

Don't forget to:
- plan your writing before you start—make a list of important points you wish to make
- write in correctly formed sentences and take care with paragraphing
- choose your words carefully, and pay attention to your spelling and punctuation
- write neatly but don't waste time
- quickly check your persuasive text once you have finished—your position must be clear to the reader.

Remember: the stance taken in a persuasive text is not wrong, as long as the writer has evidence to support his or her opinion. How the opinion is supported is as important as the opinion itself.

Start writing here.

_____

_____

_____

_____

_____

_____

_____

☞ **Marking guide on pages 133-134**

What's next ?

Week

2

This is what we cover this week:

Day 1 **Number and Algebra/**
Measurement and Geometry: ◎ Fractions, percentages and time
Measurement and Geometry: ◎ 2D shapes, 3D shapes and position

Day 2 **Spelling:** ◎ Adding 'ing' or 'ed' to verbs
◎ Common misspellings
Grammar and Punctuation: ◎ Types of nouns and adjectives

Day 3 **Reading:** ◎ Interpreting visual texts
◎ Understanding poetry

Day 4 **Writing:** ◎ Recounts

NUMBER AND ALGEBRA/ MEASUREMENT AND GEOMETRY
Fractions, percentages and time

20 MIN

Circle the correct answer.

FRACTIONS AND PERCENTAGES

1 How many thirds are there in one whole?
A 1   B 2   C 3   D 10

2 Half of 22 = ?
A 2   B 10   C 11   D 13

3 Half of 7 = ?
A 3   B $3\frac{1}{2}$ C 4   D $4\frac{1}{2}$

4 $\frac{1}{4} + \frac{1}{2} = ?$
A 1 whole   B $\frac{2}{6}$
C $\frac{3}{4}$ D 2 wholes

5 How many tenths are there in 2 wholes?
A 5   B 10   C 12   D 20

6 $\frac{1}{2} + \frac{1}{2} + \frac{1}{2} = ?$
A $\frac{1}{6}$ B $\frac{3}{6}$ C $1\frac{1}{2}$ D $2\frac{1}{2}$

7 In a test, Sandy got 5 spelling words right out of 10. What percentage did she get right?
A 50%   B 25%   C 15%   D 5%

8 What fraction of this shape is **not** shaded?

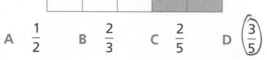

A $\frac{1}{2}$ B $\frac{2}{3}$ C $\frac{2}{5}$ D $\frac{3}{5}$

9 Levi got 75% in a Maths test. How much more did he need to receive full marks?
A 5%   B 25%   C 35%   D 100%

10 Which statement is correct?
A $\frac{3}{4} > \frac{1}{4}$ B $\frac{1}{5} > \frac{1}{2}$
C $\frac{1}{2} < \frac{1}{10}$ D $\frac{1}{3} < \frac{1}{10}$

TIME

1 James started his homework at 4:15 and finished 30 minutes later. At what time did he finish?
A 5:15   B 5 o'clock
C 4:30   D quarter to 5

2 Mr Brown worked for two weeks without a break. How many days was this?
A 7   B 9   C 10   D 14

3 What is the fifth month after April?
A August   B September
C October   D November

4 Jemima was born in 1992. How old was she on her birthday in 2006?
A 12   B 13   C 14   D 15

5 What is the time shown on this clock?
A 10 past 9
B quarter past 1
C quarter to 2
D 3 past 9

6 A 24-hour clock shows the time as 1300. What time is this on an analogue clock?
A 1 am   B 1 pm   C 11 pm   D 3 am

7 How many days are there in winter in Australia each year?
A 90   B 91   C 92   D 93

8 Both Mr and Mrs Buddle were born in 1900. Mrs Buddle lived 13 years longer than her husband, who died in 1981. When did Mrs Buddle die?
A 1994   B 1995   C 1984   D 1968

9 This is the time on a digital alarm clock How else can this time be expressed?

2:40

A 20 to 2   B 20 to 3
C quarter to 2   D 10 to 3

☞ **Explanations on pages 134–135**

Key Points

NUMBER AND ALGEBRA/ MEASUREMENT AND GEOMETRY
Fractions, percentages and time

FRACTIONS AND PERCENTAGES

1 **A fraction** is any **part of a whole**. A common fraction is written with a numerator over a denominator:

$$\frac{3}{5} \quad \frac{\text{numerator}}{\text{denominator}}$$

This fraction means 3 parts out of 5 equal parts.

2 Fractions can be located on a **number line**. Here, half is located on a number line:

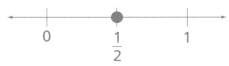

3 A **percentage** is a special fraction that is always out of 100 $\left(\text{e.g. } \frac{50}{100} = 50\%\right)$.

4 This table shows the relationships between some common fractions: halves, quarters, eighths, fifths and tenths.

One whole									
$\frac{1}{2}$					$\frac{1}{2}$				
$\frac{1}{4}$		$\frac{1}{4}$		$\frac{1}{4}$		$\frac{1}{4}$			
$\frac{1}{8}$	$\frac{1}{8}$	$\frac{1}{8}$	$\frac{1}{8}$	$\frac{1}{8}$	$\frac{1}{8}$	$\frac{1}{8}$	$\frac{1}{8}$		
$\frac{1}{5}$		$\frac{1}{5}$		$\frac{1}{5}$		$\frac{1}{5}$		$\frac{1}{5}$	
$\frac{1}{10}$	$\frac{1}{10}$	$\frac{1}{10}$	$\frac{1}{10}$	$\frac{1}{10}$	$\frac{1}{10}$	$\frac{1}{10}$	$\frac{1}{10}$	$\frac{1}{10}$	$\frac{1}{10}$

5 This table shows some **common fractions** and **the percentages** they amount to.

$\frac{1}{10}$			10%
$\frac{2}{10}$	$\frac{1}{5}$		20%
$\frac{1}{4}$			25%
$\frac{3}{10}$			30%
$\frac{4}{10}$	$\frac{2}{5}$		40%
$\frac{5}{10}$	$\frac{2}{4}$	$\frac{1}{2}$	50%
$\frac{6}{10}$	$\frac{3}{5}$		60%
$\frac{7}{10}$			70%
$\frac{3}{4}$			75%
$\frac{8}{10}$	$\frac{4}{5}$		80%
$\frac{9}{10}$			90%
$\frac{10}{10}$	$\frac{5}{5}$		100%

6 You should be able to **work out fractions of a whole**.

Example: What fraction of this shape is shaded?

Two parts out of six, or $\frac{2}{6} = \frac{1}{3}$.

TIME

1 Learn your **time facts**!

> 60 seconds = 1 minute
> 60 minutes = 1 hour
> 24 hours = 1 day
> 7 days = 1 week
> 12 months = 1 year
> 52 weeks = 1 year
> 365 days = 1 year
> 366 days = 1 leap year
> 1 century = 100 years

**NUMBER AND ALGEBRA/
MEASUREMENT AND GEOMETRY**
Fractions, percentages and time

2 Know the **days of the week** (Monday, Tuesday, Wednesday, Thursday, Friday, Saturday, Sunday) and the months of the year (January, February, March, April, May, June, July, August, September, October, November, December).

Know how many **days in each month**.

Months with **30 days**: April, June, September, November

Months with **31 days**: January, March, May, July, August, October, December

Months with **28 days**: February (except for leap years when it has 29 days)

To work out what the **date will be** one **week after 28 November**:

2 days (November has 30 days) + 5 days = 5 December.

3 **Leap years** are every four years. The next leap year after 2008 is 2012.

4 **The day is divided into am** and **pm**: am refers to that part of a day between midnight and noon, and pm is the time between noon and midnight:

half past 6 in the morning = 6:30 am.

These labels are only used with 12-hour time.

5 In **twenty-four hour time one day** is divided into 24 parts to avoid confusion between am and pm times.

12-hour time	24-hour time
1 am	0100 (01:00)
10 am	1000 (10:00)
12 noon	1200 (12:00)
2 pm	1400 (14:00)
12 midnight	0000 (00:00)

6 The months are divided into **four seasons**.

Summer	Autumn
December	March
January	April
February	May
Winter	Spring
June	September
July	October
August	November

7 Here is a simple conversion between **analog and digital time**:

Quarter past 4 = 4:15

Real Test

NUMBER AND ALGEBRA/ MEASUREMENT AND GEOMETRY
Fractions, percentages and time

20 MIN

1 Vincent drew a number line.

What number is the arrow pointing to?

A $\frac{1}{2}$ B $\frac{3}{4}$ C $2\frac{1}{2}$ D $3\frac{1}{2}$

2 What is one quarter of 12?

A $\frac{4}{12}$ B 3   C 4   D 48

3 What is the largest fraction?

A $\frac{1}{4}$ B $\frac{1}{3}$ C $\frac{1}{2}$ D $\frac{1}{8}$

4 What fraction of the shape is shaded?

A $\frac{4}{9}$ B $\frac{1}{2}$

C $\frac{5}{9}$ D $\frac{2}{3}$

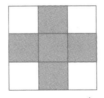

5 The diagram contains hearts:

What fraction of the hearts in the diagram are shaded?

A $\frac{1}{8}$ B $\frac{1}{4}$ C $\frac{1}{2}$ D $\frac{4}{7}$

6 Jayden scored 82% in his test. How much more did he need to score full marks?

A 18%   B 28%
C 22%   D 32%

7 Sumalee exercised each morning for 20 minutes. After 5 days what was the total time she had exercised?

A 1 hr 20 min   B 1 hr 30 min
C 1 hr 40 min   D 1 hr 50 min

8 What is the time on the analog clock?

A 2:45
B 3:15
C 3:45
D 4:15

9 Today is Tuesday 16th June. What day of the week is 27th June?

A Saturday   B Sunday
C Monday   D Wednesday

10 A movie commenced at 4:20 pm and lasted for $1\frac{1}{2}$ hours. What time did the movie finish?

A 5:20 pm   B 5:40 pm
C 5:50 pm   D 6:00 pm

11 Brendan visited his grandmother from 11:30 am to 1:00 pm. How long was his visit?

A 30 min   B 1 hr 30 min
C 2 hr 30 min   D 3 hr 30 min

12 Training lasts an hour and is about to commence in 5 minutes. If it is now 4:10 pm, what time will training finish?

A 4:15 pm   B 5:10 pm
C 5:15 pm   D 5:30 pm

13 Dinh's birthday is in 12 days. If today is 24th May, what date is his birthday?

A 4th June   B 5th June
C 6th June   D 7th June

14 Phoebe can read a page of her novel in 2 minutes. How many pages will she read in half an hour?

A 15 pages   B 20 pages
C 30 pages   D 60 pages

15 A television show commenced at 3:15 pm and finished at 3:55 pm. How long did the television show run?

A 30 minutes   B 40 minutes
C 45 minutes   D 50 minutes

16 Jackson was born in June 1998. In what year will Jackson turn 25?

A 2023   B 2024
C 2025   D 2027

☞ **Answers and explanations on pages 135–136**

MEASUREMENT AND GEOMETRY
2D shapes, 3D shapes and position

20 MIN

Circle the correct answer.

2D SHAPES

1 Which shape is the rectangle?

 A B C D

2 Which shape contains parallel lines?

 A B C D

3 Here are four angles. Which angle is the right angle?

 A B C D

4 How many sides does a hexagon have?
  A 3   B 4   C 6   D 8

5 Which line is perpendicular to the dark line?

  A   B ——— C   D

6 This shape was rotated a quarter turn clockwise. What does the shape look like?

 A   B

  C   D

3D SHAPES

1 Which shape is the cylinder?

  A   B
  C   D

2 How many cubes are there in this stack?
  A 9   B 10
  C 15   D 18

3 What shape can be made from this net?
  A cube
  B triangular prism
  C square pyramid
  D rectangular prism

4 What would this tower look like from above?

  A   B

  C   D

5 Indira has a tennis ball. A tennis ball is most like
  A a circle.   B a cone.
  C a sphere.   D an oval.

6 This shape is cut in half as shown by the dotted line. What shape will the cut faces be most like?

  A   B

  C   D

☞ **Explanations on page 136**

Key Points

MEASUREMENT AND GEOMETRY
2D shapes, 3D shapes and position

2D SHAPES

1 **Types of triangles**

right-angled
(contains a right-angle)

isosceles
(2 sides, 2 angles equal)

equilateral
(all sides and angles equal)

2 **Basic quadrilateral shapes** (4-sided)

rectangle　square　kite　parallelogram

3 **Hexagons** have 6 sides.
Octagons have 8 sides.

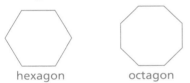

hexagon　octagon

4 **Types of lines**

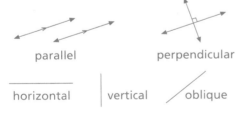

parallel　perpendicular

horizontal　vertical　oblique

5 **Types of angles** (an angle has two arms)

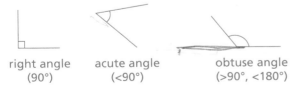

right angle
(90°)

acute angle
(<90°)

obtuse angle
(>90°, <180°)

6 **Diagonals** are lines that join the corners of 2D shapes.
A square has 2 diagonals.
A triangle has no diagonals.

7 **Tessellating shapes** are shapes that fit together without gaps or overlapping.

Squares tessellate

Circles do not tessellate

8 2D shapes can be **flipped**, **slid** or **turned**. This arrow is flipped.

9 Some **shapes are symmetrical**. A rectangle has 2 axes of symmetry. Axes are often called mirror lines.

3D SHAPES

1 **3D shapes** include:

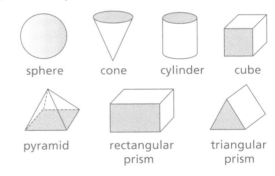

sphere　cone　cylinder　cube

pyramid　rectangular prism　triangular prism

2 The **features of 3D shapes** are **faces**, **edges** and **vertices** (corners). A cube has 6 faces, 12 edges and 8 vertices. Faces must be flat. Surfaces can be curved or flat.

3 Some questions may ask you to **visualise** (imagine) **3D shapes from other positions**. A square pyramid as viewed from above would look like this:

Key Points

MEASUREMENT AND GEOMETRY
2D shapes, 3D shapes and position

4 You may also be asked to **count all the blocks** in a stack when all blocks are not visible.
There are four blocks in this stack.

5 A **cross-section** is the shape that is made when a solid shape is cut straight through. When the top is cut off a cone (parallel to the base), the shape of the new face will look like a circle:

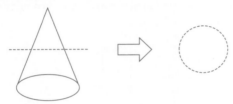

6 It is important to recognise **3D shapes** in the **environment**. A soccer ball is much like a sphere.

POSITION

1 The **location of an object** can be described by its position in a row and in a column. For example, the X in the grid below is in position C3.

4				
3			✕	
2				
1				
	A	B	C	D

2 The **position of an object** can be described as a relationship to other objects. In the example below, the peaches are on the bottom row, second from the left.

Top row	apples	oranges	bananas	pineapples
Bottom row	lemons	peaches	mangoes	passionfruit

3 A **compass rose** can be used to describe the direction from one position to another. For example, in the diagram below, point B is south-east of point A.

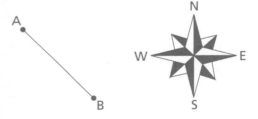

Real Test

MEASUREMENT AND GEOMETRY
2D shapes, 3D shapes and position

20 MIN

1 What is the name of this shape?
- A triangle
- B hexagon
- C pentagon
- D trapezium

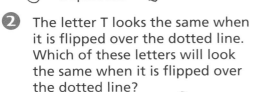

2 The letter T looks the same when it is flipped over the dotted line. Which of these letters will look the same when it is flipped over the dotted line?
- A C
- B M
- C Z
- D P

T

3 Melinda drew a shape with eight sides. What shape did she draw?
- A parallelogram
- B octagon
- C hexagon
- D pentagon

4 How many lines of symmetry can be drawn on the shape?
- A 1
- B 2
- C 3
- D 4

5 Which of the following letters does not have one pair of parallel lines?
- A F
- B Z
- C O
- D H

6 How many rectangles are there in this shape?
- A 3
- B 4
- C 5
- D 6

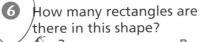

7 How many faces are on this solid?
- A 4
- B 5
- C 6
- D 8

8 What is the name of this shape?
- A triangular prism
- B cone
- C sphere
- D cylinder

9 How many edges are on a cube?
- A 6
- B 8
- C 9
- D 12

10 This is a sketch of a rectangular pyramid. What is the top view of the solid?

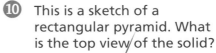

- A
- B
- C
- D

11 Sam sketched the net of a triangular prism using triangles and some rectangles. How many rectangles did she use?
- A 3
- B 4
- C 5
- D 6

12 A cylinder is cut in half as shown by the dotted line. What shape will the cut faces be most like?

- A
- B
- C
- D

13 Joanne has a tin of tomatoes in her pantry. What shape is the tin?
- A sphere
- B cylinder
- C triangular prism
- D cube

14 Guy is standing at Z. What direction is the bookshop?
- A south-east
- B south-west
- C north-east
- D north-west

chemist — Z — bank

newsagency   bookshop

15 If Laura is on the bottom row, who is second from the right on the top row?

Tom	Brad	Sam	Lee
Ian	Laura	Rick	Jan

- A Tom
- B Brad
- C Sam
- D Rick

16 What is the location of P on the grid?
- A A3
- B B2
- C B3
- D C2

3		P	
2			
1			
	A	B	C	D

☞ **Answers and explanations on pages 136-137**

SPELLING
Adding 'ing' or 'ed' to verbs

 With most spelling rules there are exceptions. English words have many different origins (e.g. 'bunyip' comes from Aboriginal Australian and 'marathon' comes from Greece).

Key Points

1 With most words you simply add 'ing' or 'ed'.
Examples: bowl → bowling, bowled; hand → handing, handed; boot → booting, booted

2 a For words that end with a consonant + 'y', simply add 'ing'.
Examples: spy → spying, bury → burying, supply → supplying

  b When adding 'ed' to words that end in a consonant + 'y', change the 'y' to 'i' before adding 'ed'.
Examples: tally → tallied, fry → fried, hurry → hurried

3 For words ending with a consonant + 'e', drop the 'e' and then add 'ing' or 'ed'.
Examples: hope → hoping, hoped; dine → dining, dined; wave → waving, waved

4 For words ending in a single vowel + a consonant, simply double the last letter before adding 'ing'.
Examples: hop → hopping, hopped; skip → skipping, skipped; beg → begging, begged

Main exceptions are words ending in 'w', 'x' and 'y'.
Examples: show → showing, showed; tax → taxing, taxed; stay → staying, stayed

Test Your Skills

Learn the words below. A common method of learning and self-testing is the LOOK, SAY, COVER, WRITE, CHECK method. If you make any mistakes, you should rewrite the word three times correctly, immediately. This is so you will become familiar with the correct spelling. If the word is especially difficult, rewrite it several more times or keep a list of words that you can check regularly.

This week's theme word: SHOPPING

shop	_____	money	_____
shopping	_____	cash	_____
shopped	_____	display	_____
pay	_____	displayed	_____
paying	_____	displaying	_____
paid	_____	buy	_____
cross	_____	buying	_____
crossing	_____	seek	_____
crossed	_____	seeking	_____
mall	_____	trade	_____
market	_____	trading	_____
shelf	_____	traded	_____

Write any troublesome words three times: _____ _____ _____

_____ _____ _____

Real Test

1 The spelling mistakes in these sentences have been highlighted.
Write the correct spelling for each highlighted word in the box.

a Justine got a lofe of bread at the supermarket.

b Don't use the brome to sweep up scraps!

c Do we wear broun or black ribbons?

d We have a new brix house with a tile roof.

e When did you last come your hair?

f The dog barkt at the children in the street.

g Meg was smileing when I took her picture.

h The school cleanner starts work at six o'clock.

2 The spelling mistakes in these labels have been highlighted.
Write the correct spelling for each highlighted word in the correct box.

a handel

b stele frame

c frount

d whele

3 Read the text *Dolphins*.
Each line has a word that is incorrect. Write the correct spelling of the word in the box.

Dolphins

a Some dolphins look a bit like wales but

b are mush smaller. Their snout is like

c a beek and the fin on their back is

d shaped like a hook. Thay have powerful

e flippers and a flat tail. Dolphins seem too talk

f to each other by makeing different sounds.

☞ **Answers on page 137**

Key Points and Test Your Skills

GRAMMAR AND PUNCTUATION
Types of nouns and adjectives

15 MIN

Key Points

1 Here are two important types of nouns.

a Common nouns are the names of everyday things around us.
Examples: boat, cat, roads, web, dinosaur, jungle

b Proper nouns begin with a capital letter and are the names of particular persons, places or things.
Examples: Sunday, Adelaide, Holden, Kings Park, Boxing Day, Fijians

2 **a** Adjectives are words that tell us more about nouns or describe them.
Examples: dirty hands, cold wind, ten toes, black shoes, the grass is soft

b Proper adjectives are formed from proper nouns.
Examples: Italy → Italian, France → French

c Adjectives have three degrees of comparison.
Example: Rita is old. (One person is old.)
Bill is older than Rita. (Two people are compared.)
Charlie is the oldest person in the group. (Three or more people are compared.)

d Many adjectives have opposites—words with an opposite meaning.
Examples: wet → dry, young → old, happy → sad

Test Your Skills

1 Name the types of nouns.

a Perth *proper noun*   friend *common*   clouds *common*

b ice *common*   enemy *common*   King George *proper*

c leg *common*   explosion *common*   Murray River *proper*

d Martian *proper*   alien *common*   moon *common*

2 Draw a line under the adjectives in these sentences.

a <u>Strong</u> winds blew <u>small</u> yachts into <u>wild</u> seas.

b <u>Broken</u> glass, <u>rusty</u> tins and smelly rags filled the <u>battered</u> bin.

3 Write the correct word in the space.

a Frank is _stronger_ than his brother. (strong, stronger, strongest)

b My grandfather is the _oldest_ person in my family. (old, older, oldest)

c Who is the _fastest_ person in the world? (fast, faster, fastest)

d It is _drier_ at our place than at your place. (dry, drier, driest)

4 Write the opposites for these words.

a ugly _pretty_   **b** rough _easy / smooth_   **c** dirty _clean_

d young _old_

GRAMMAR AND PUNCTUATION
Types of nouns and adjectives

15 MIN

1 Which of the following correctly completes this sentence?

We will catch the next train because it [____] at all the stations.

stop	stops	stopping	stopped
A	B	C	D

2 Which of the following correctly completes this sentence?

The ball was [____] by Olivia on the sideline.

catched	catch	caught	caughted
A	B	C	D

3 Which of the following correctly completes this sentence?

Although Natalie is younger than Tricia she is still the [____] in Group A.

oldest	older	most old	old
A	B	C	D

4 Which of the following correctly completes this sentence?

Every summer is hot but winters are the opposite. They are [____].

warm	cool	cold	cloudy
A	B	C	D

5 Which of the following correctly completes this sentence?

[____] you have been hard working you can have a little reward.

Either	Because	But	Yet
A	B	C	D

6 Which of the following correctly completes this sentence?

Mr Hughes came to the classroom to [____] the students road safety.

teach	learn	taught	teached
A	B	C	D

7 Which sentence has the correct punctuation?
A Most people who live in France are French.
B Most people who live in France are french.
C Most People who live in France are French.
D Most people who live in france are French.

Read the text *Travels*. The text has some gaps. Choose the best option to fill each gap.

Travels

I love travelling.

Have you ever been to [____] It is great.

8

Italy	italy.	Italy.	Italy?
A	B	C	D

Italians enjoy life. They enjoy [____] daily life

9

there	their	Their	There
A	B	C	D

☞ **Answers and explanations on pages 137–138**

cup _____ coffee and a talk while playing a

card game. _____ the south there are high

volcanoes and islands that _____

surrounded by clear, blue _____

10
ov	per	off	of
A	B	C	(D) ✓

11
at	On	In	in
(A)	B	(C)	D ✓

12
are	is	do	was
(A)	B	C	D ✓

13
water	water!	Water	water.
A	B	C	(D) ✓

14 Which sentence has the correct punctuation?
(A) On Friday we went to the library before having lunch in Belmont park.
B On friday we went to the library before having lunch in Belmont Park.
C On Friday we went to the Library before having lunch in belmont park.
(D) On Friday we went to the library before having lunch in Belmont Park. ✓

15 Which of the following correctly completes the sentence?

There was so _____ sand in my shoes I could have made a beach! ✓

more	much	many	most
A	(B)	C	D

16 Shade a bubble to show where the missing question mark (?) should go.

How far can you count I can count by tens to one hundred.

(A)   (B)   C   D   ✓

17 Which sentence has the correct punctuation?
(A) The strangers shoe's were full of holes and without laces.
B The strangers shoes were full of hole's and without laces.
(C) The stranger's shoes were full of holes and without laces. ✓
(D) The stranger's shoe's were full of hole's and without lace's.

18 Which word is unnecessary in this sentence?

The elephant was standing in the river lifting up heavy logs.
A standing
B lifting
(C) up ✓
D heavy

☞ **Answers and explanations on pages 137–138**

Stories can be told in pictures as well as just words. Films and comics are examples of this. Study this simple cartoon about two donkeys then answer the questions. Each part of the story is set in a frame. You will have to use your imagination to understand what is happening. Circle the correct answers.

1. What are the donkeys doing in the first three frames? They are trying to
   A escape.
   B reach something.
   C break a rope.
   D have a tug-o-war.

2. What does the question mark (?) in Frame 4 suggest?
   A The donkeys realise they have a problem.
   B One donkey wants to ask a question.
   C The donkeys are talking about having a rest.
   D The donkeys think about another game.

3. In Frame 6, one pile of food has disappeared. What has happened to it?
   A The owner took it away.   B It was eaten by one of the donkeys.
   C It was eaten by both donkeys.   D It was put with the other pile of food.

4. Frame 6 shows that the donkeys are most likely feeling
   A exhausted.   B angry.   C puzzled.   D happy.

5. In Frame 1, there are lines near each donkey's nose. These suggest that the donkeys are
   A sneezing.   B sniffing.   C shouting.   D snuffling.

6. What lesson does the illustration suggest?
   A Two heads are better than one.   B Ask no questions and be told no lies.
   C Waste not, want not.   D Sharing is better than arguing.

☞ **Explanations on page 138**

Real Test

READING
Interpreting visual texts

8 MIN

Many small businesses distribute information about their services or products through 'mail drops'. These are usual half-page fliers, sometimes referred to as 'junk mail'.
Study this flier, 'Play, play, play!', and answer the questions. Circle the correct answers.

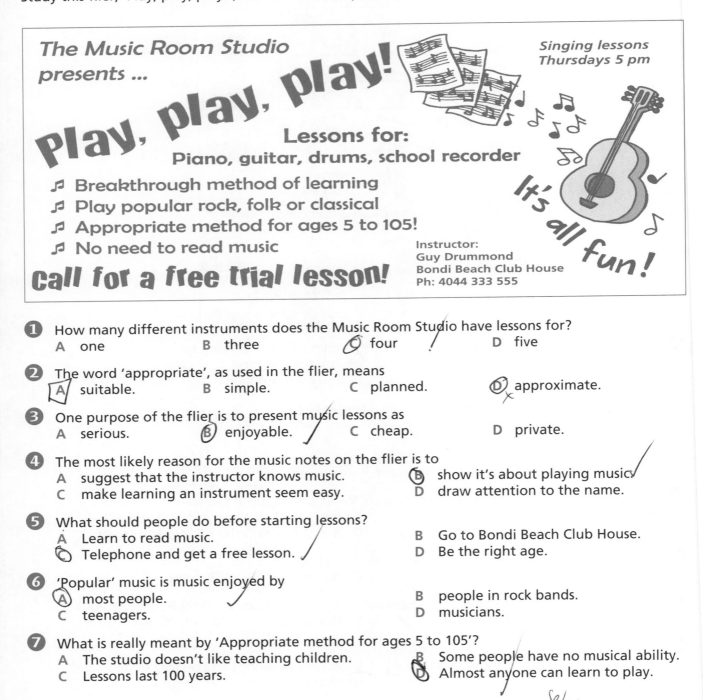

The Music Room Studio presents ...

Singing lessons
Thursdays 5 pm

Play, play, play!

Lessons for:
Piano, guitar, drums, school recorder

♪ Breakthrough method of learning
♪ Play popular rock, folk or classical
♪ Appropriate method for ages 5 to 105!
♪ No need to read music

call for a free trial lesson!

Instructor:
Guy Drummond
Bondi Beach Club House
Ph: 4044 333 555

It's all fun!

1 How many different instruments does the Music Room Studio have lessons for?
A one   B three   C four   D five

2 The word 'appropriate', as used in the flier, means
A suitable.   B simple.   C planned.   D approximate.

3 One purpose of the flier is to present music lessons as
A serious.   B enjoyable.   C cheap.   D private.

4 The most likely reason for the music notes on the flier is to
A suggest that the instructor knows music.   B show it's about playing music.
C make learning an instrument seem easy.   D draw attention to the name.

5 What should people do before starting lessons?
A Learn to read music.   B Go to Bondi Beach Club House.
C Telephone and get a free lesson.   D Be the right age.

6 'Popular' music is music enjoyed by
A most people.   B people in rock bands.
C teenagers.   D musicians.

7 What is really meant by 'Appropriate method for ages 5 to 105'?
A The studio doesn't like teaching children.   B Some people have no musical ability.
C Lessons last 100 years.   D Almost anyone can learn to play.

☞ **Answers and explanations on page 138**

READING
Understanding poetry

7 min

A poem can take many forms. It can tell a story, paint a word picture, or be made into a play. Poets create experiences that are shared with the reader. They choose their words carefully. They create images and feelings with words. To do this, they use techniques such as **figurative language** (including similes and metaphors), rhyme and different rhythms—but remember that poetry does not have to rhyme.

 The person who writes the poem is called the **poet**. The person who seems to be saying the poem is called the **narrator**. The narrator uses such words as **I** and **me** when speaking about himself or herself.

Read the poem 'My Cat' by Elaine Horsfield and answer the questions. Circle the correct answer.

My Cat

My cat looks like a cotton ball
All white and fluffy fur.
She feels so soft and silky
When I sit and play with her.

I know she's ready for her tea
When I come home from school,
I hear her meow and make a fuss
Then jump up on her stool.

Before she eats she smells her meat
That I put in her dish.
Sometimes I feed her chicken wings
And other days it's fish.

She eats her food with tiny bites,
I'm sure she likes the taste,
She licks the bowl until it's clean
There's never any waste.

1 This poem
  A tells a story.
  C describes a pet.
  B explains a problem.
  D describes a scene.

2 Which word rhymes with 'waste'?
  A taste
  B wings
  C clean
  D bites

3 Which term best describes the pet owner?
  A fussy
  B caring
  C bothered
  D lazy

4 A 'fluffy' cat would be
  A heavy to nurse.
  C smooth to pat.
  B soft and cuddly.
  D dark and shiny.

5 What does the cat do before she eats her meat?
  A licks her whiskers
  C cleans the bowl
  B jumps on a stool
  D smells the meat

6 Choose the statement about the pet cat that is true.
  A The pet cat gets excited when the owner comes home.
  B The pet cat doesn't like chicken wings.
  C The pet cat is messy when she eats her food.
  D The pet cat spends all day playing with cotton balls.

Real Test

Read the poem 'Clean Your Room!' by Elaine Horsfield and answer the questions.

Clean Your Room!

When my mum gets up in the morning
She first of all makes up the bed.
Then she scrubs out the shower
For at least half an hour,
And makes sure the family is fed.

And after she's cleared up the dishes,
And washed all the plates and the mugs,
She gets out the broom
And sweeps out each room,
Then shakes out the dust from the rugs.

But as soon as she gets to my bedroom,
It's 'Katie, you've not made your bed.
And just look at this floor,
And the mess by the door!
Put that book down and clean up instead!'

So I sigh as I fold up my T-shirts,
And pick up my books and my pens.
'Cause I know once it's clean,
And Mum's been in and seen,
It will only get dirty again!

1 This poem
  A tells a story.
  B looks at a problem a child has.
  C describes a landscape.
  D explains an amusing event.

2 The word 'cleared' is used in the poem. Which word has a similar meaning?
  A collected   B washed
  C dried   D stacked

3 How does Katie feel about tidying her room? She feels it is
  A important.   B necessary.
  C difficult.   D useless.

4 What does Katie expect her mother to do after Katie has tidied her room?
  A the washing up   B inspect the room
  C read a book   D give Katie another task

5 The last line of the poem suggests that
  A Katie sees no point in cleaning the room.
  B it is important to keep the house tidy.
  C Katie is a lazy, selfish person.
  D Katie's mother is very unfair.

6 What does Katie prefer to do instead of cleaning her room?
  A fold her T-shirts   B help her mother
  C read a book   D tidy her desk

7 Write the numbers 1, 2, 3 and 4 in the boxes to show the order in which Katie's mother did things.

  ☐ scrubs the shower   ☐ makes the bed   ☐ shakes the rugs   ☐ feeds the family

☞ Explanations on page 139

Real Test

Read the poem 'Quiet Please!' by Elaine Horsfield and answer the questions.

Note: Remember, the person who writes the poem is called the poet. The person who seems to be saying the poem is called the narrator. The narrator uses such words as 'I' and 'me' when speaking about him- or herself.

Quiet Please!

Quiet please! There's a baby in the house.
Everyone is tip-toe-ing as quietly as a mouse.
Quiet please! She's only just asleep
If you must go near her room
You really have to creep.

Quiet please! The TV's turned down low,
Nintendo games are out of bounds. But what I'd like to know,
Is why we must be quiet, and not play with our toys
And how come she's the only one
Allowed to make a noise?

---

1 Where is the setting for this poem?
 A in a home
 C in a park
 B in a school
 D in a playgroup

2 One line of the poem is: 'But what I'd like to know ...'. Who is most likely saying this line?
 A the baby
 C a friend
 B the mother or father
 D a sister or brother

3 How does the narrator feel about being told to keep quiet?
 A surprised
 C unfairly treated
 B amused
 D trapped

4 What is the most likely reason the poet has used an exclamation mark (!) after 'Quiet please!'?
 A to show that an adult is making an order
 B members of the family are being noisy
 C the baby is crying loudly
 D someone is sneaking into the baby's room

5 Which word in the poem rhymes with creep? Write your answer on the line.

---

6 Which statement is true?
 A The TV is keeping the baby awake.
 C The baby has just gone to sleep.
 B The baby is asleep in the TV room.
 D The baby has to be kept quiet.

7 What action is banned?
 A watching TV
 C tip-toe-ing around the house
 B playing Nintendo games
 D going near the baby's bedroom

☞ **Answers and explanations on page 139**

TIPS FOR WRITING RECOUNTS

A **recount** tells about events that have happened to you or other people. The purpose of a factual recount is to record a series of events in the order they happened and evaluate their importance in some way. A recount can also be fictitious. Whether the recount is factual or fictitious remember to tell who, what, when, where and why. There are many types of recount—diaries, newspaper reports, letters and biographies. Recounts can be the easiest texts to write if you are given the choice. They don't need much planning or organisation as they are a straightforward record of events.

When writing recounts it is best to keep these points in mind. They will help you get the best possible mark.

Before you start writing

- Read the question and check the stimulus material carefully. *Stimulus material* means the topic, title, picture, words, phrases or extract of writing you are given to base your writing on.
- Remember that a recount is usually told in the past tense because the events described have already happened.
- Write about something you know. Don't try to write about something way outside your experience.
- Use a setting you are familiar with, e.g. home, school, sport, holiday place or shopping centre.
- When you have chosen your topic it might be helpful to jot down a few ideas quickly on paper so you don't forget them. Make up your mind quickly if you are writing a first-person recount (using *I* as the main character) or a third-person recount. If it is a personal recount, try to avoid too many sentences beginning with *I*.

The introduction

- A striking title gives impact to a recount. Newspaper reports do this well.

The body

- **Use conjunctions and connectives**, e.g. *when, then, first* or *next*. Because recounts can record either events that happen over a short period or events that happen over a lifetime, you need conjunctions and connectives to link and order the events.
- **Correctly paragraph your writing.** You need a new paragraph when there is a change in time or place, or a new idea. You may want to comment on the events as you write about them.
- **Include personal comments**, e.g. about your feelings, your opinions and your reactions, but only include comments that add to your recount. 'Waffle' and unnecessary detail don't improve a recount. It is better to stick to the facts without getting sidetracked.
- **Use language imaginatively** so that the recount is interesting, but don't try to fill it with weird or disgusting events.

The conclusion

- **Include a conclusion**. This tells how the experience ended. You may give your opinion about what happened and some thoughts you may have had about it. This final comment on the events or experiences is a way to wrap up your recount.

When you have finished writing give yourself a few moments to read through your recount. Quickly check spelling and punctuation, and insert words that have been accidentally left out.

Real Test and Tips

There is no way of knowing for certain what type of writing will be included in NAPLAN tests in years to come. This is an opportunity for you to practise different types of writing.

Before you start, read the General writing tips on pages 20–21 and the Tips for writing recounts on page 46.

A recount tells about events that have happened to you or other people. It is usually a record of events as they have happened. Events are told in order. A recount can conclude with a personal opinion of the event.

Today you are going to write a personal recount of A SCHOOL EXCURSION. Think about where you went for the excursion and how you got there. Was it by bus or by train, by car or were you able to walk? A school excursion can be to a sporting event or the town library. It can be just a few hours long or it could be an overnight excursion. Did anything unusual happen on the way? How did people react? How did you feel about the excursion? In what way was it a success or fun? Did anything happen to make the excursion less pleasant?

Before you start writing, give some thought to:
- where your recount takes place
- the characters and what they do in your recount
- the events that take place in your recount and the problems that have to be resolved
- how you, and others, felt about the excursion—you may comment on events as you write about them.

Don't forget to:
- plan your recount before you start writing
- write in correctly formed sentences and take care with paragraphing
- choose your words carefully and pay attention to your spelling and punctuation
- write neatly but don't waste time
- quickly check your recount once you have finished.

Start writing here.

_____

_____

_____

_____

_____

_____

_____

_____

☞ **Marking guide on page 140**

Real Test and Tips

WRITING
Recount 2

40 MIN

There is no way of knowing for certain what type of writing will be included in NAPLAN tests in years to come. This is an opportunity for you to practise different types of writing.

Before you start, read the General writing tips on pages 20–21 and the Tips for writing recounts on page 46.

A recount tells about events that have happened to you or other people. It is usually a record of events as they have happened. Events are told in order. A recount can conclude with a personal opinion of the event.

Today you are going to write a personal recount about A HOT DAY or A COLD DAY. Think about a day when it was hotter or colder than usual. What did you do about it? How did things change during the day? Did you go to the beach or build a snowman? How did the weather make you feel? Think about what you did to make yourself feel comfortable. Think about what you had to wear, and how you protected yourself against the sun or the cold. How did other people react? Was there a sudden change in the weather late in the day?

Before you start writing, give some thought to:
- where your recount takes place
- the characters and what they do in your recount
- the events that take place in your recount and the problems that have to be resolved
- how you, and others, reacted to the extreme weather—you may comment on events as you write about them.

Don't forget to:
- plan your recount before you start writing
- write in correctly formed sentences and take care with paragraphing
- choose your words carefully and pay attention to your spelling and punctuation
- write neatly but don't waste time
- quickly check your recount once you have finished.

Start writing here.

_____

_____

_____

_____

_____

_____

_____

_____

☞ **Marking guide on pages 140-141**

We're halfway there!

Week 3

This is what we cover this week:

Day 1   **Measurement and Geometry:**   ◎ Length, mass and capacity
                                       ◎ Area and volume

Day 2   **Spelling:**   ◎ 'ie' and 'ei' words and the suffix 'ful'
                        ◎ Common misspellings
         Grammar and Punctuation: ◎ Commas, verbs, tense and 'agreement'

Day 3   **Reading:**   ◎ Understanding recounts
                      ◎ Understanding explanations

Day 4   **Writing:**   ◎ Narrative texts

Test Your Skills

MEASUREMENT AND GEOMETRY
Length, mass and capacity

20 MIN

LENGTH

1 What is the best measure for the length of a soccer field?
- A metres
- B centimetres ✓
- C millimetres
- D kilometres

2 Len is sitting on a chair at a dining room table. About how high is the seat of the chair from the floor?
- A 10 cm
- B 40 cm ✓
- C 150 cm
- D 80 cm

3 How many centimetres are there in 2.5 m?
- A 25
- B 205
- C 250
- D 2500

4 What is the perimeter of a 5 cm square?
- A 5 cm
- B 10 cm
- C 20 cm
- D 25 cm

5 What is the perimeter of this rectangle?
- A 15 cm
- B 21 cm
- C 24 cm
- D 30 cm ✓

9 cm
6 cm

6 Estimate the length of this line.

Its length is about
- A 8 mm.
- B 2 cm.
- C 8 cm.
- D 15 cm. ✓

7 What would be the best way to measure exactly the width of a bedroom?
- A trundle wheel
- B tape measure
- C paces
- D school ruler ✓

8 The capacity of a common bucket is about
- A 60 L.
- B 10 L.
- C 20 mL.
- D 100 L. ✓

9 Michael lives 3 km from school. How far would he travel in an average school week when travelling to and from school?
- A 6 km
- B 12 km
- C 15 km
- D 30 km

MASS AND CAPACITY

1 What is the best measure for the mass of margarine in a full tub?
- A grams
- B litres ✓
- C milligrams
- D tonnes

2 Erin's mother took 250 g of flour from a 1 kg carton. How much flour was left in the carton?
- A 50 g
- B 250 g
- C 750 g ✓
- D 1750 g

3 Mr Yuan stepped on his bathroom scales. Mr Yuan's mass is
- A 70 kg.
- B 78 kg.
- C 73 kg.
- D 80 kg.

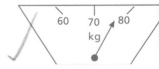

60 70 80 kg

4 A millilitre of water has a mass of one gram. What would be the mass of one litre of water?
- A 50 g
- B 100 g
- C 500 g
- D 1 kg

5 Mr Macmillan has 2.5 kg of nails. How much is this in grams?
- A 25 g
- B 250 g
- C 1250 g
- D 2500 g

6 Which of these would have a mass of about 50 g?
- A an egg
- B a cricket ball
- C a postcard
- D a tub of ice-cream

7 Three students measured their mass on the classroom scales.

| Cindy – 56 kg |
| Sammy – 43 kg |
| Leanne – 61 kg |

What is the difference in mass between the heaviest and lightest students?
- A 5 kg
- B 13 kg
- C 18 kg
- D 43 kg

☞ **Explanations on pages 141-142**

Key Points

MEASUREMENT AND GEOMETRY
Length, mass and capacity

1 In **metric units, the prefix** (the beginning of the word) tells us the size.

	Prefix	Symbol	Value	Example
smaller ↑	milli–	m	$\frac{1}{1000}$	millilitre (mL)
	centi–	c	$\frac{1}{100}$	centimetre (cm)
Basic unit (1)				
larger ↓	hecto–	h	$100 \times$	hectare (ha)
	kilo–	k	$1000 \times$	kilogram (kg

Examples: 100 centimetres = 1 metre
1000 metres = 1 kilometre
1000 grams = 1 kilogram
1000 kilograms = 1 tonne
1000 millilitres = 1 litre
1000 litres = 1 kilolitre

2 **Common measurements** using **symbols:**
1000 mL = 1 L   1000 m = 1 km
1000 L = 1 kL   1000 g = 1 kg
100 cm = 1 m   1000 kg = 1 t

3 **Capacity** is how much liquid a container can hold. **Liquids** are measured in mL, L and kL. Notice that the capital 'L' is used for litres to prevent confusion with the number '1'.

4 **Perimeter** is the distance around a 2D shape.
The perimeter of a 5 cm **square** is 20 cm. There are four sides, each 5 cm long:

5 cm

5 cm

4×5 cm = 20 cm *or*
5 cm + 5 cm + 5 cm + 5 cm = 20 cm

The perimeter of a **rectangle** is found by adding the length of all four sides. You may find it easier to double the length of the opposite sides, then add.
To find the perimeter of a rectangle
6 cm × 3 cm:

6 cm

3 cm

$(2 \times 6$ cm$) + (2 \times 3$ cm$) = 12 + 6 = 18$ cm

5 Different devices can be used to measure length, mass and capacity. Here are some examples.
Length: hand spans, paces, rulers, tapes, trundle wheels
Mass: hefting (using the open hands), balance beams, spring balances, scales
Capacity: cups, measuring jugs/beakers, milk cartons

6 **Measurements can be converted** (changed) from one form to another.
To convert kilometres to metres, kilograms to grams or kilolitres to litres, **multiply by 1000**:

7 km = 7000 m
3 kg = 3000 g

To convert metres to kilometres, grams to kilograms or millilitres to litres, **divide by 1000**:

9000 m = 9 km

You can also cross out three zeros:

5000 g = 5(000̶) kg = 5 kg

7 To **convert metre lengths** that have **two decimal places** to centimetres, simply remove the decimal point:

5.79 m = 579 cm

To reverse the operation, simple add the decimal point two places from the right-hand end:

392 cm = 3.92 m

8 **Estimating** is an important measurement skill. To make good comparisons it is useful to know the terms used and the sizes of some common objects (e.g. a litre of milk, a kilogram of butter, a long step—about 1 m, a teaspoon of medicine—5 mL, the mass of a letter—about 10 g).

Real Test

MEASUREMENT AND GEOMETRY
Length, mass and capacity

20 MIN

---

1 Which person is the tallest?

Alice Brenda Coral Deeane

A Alice
B Brenda
C Coral
D Deeane ✓

2 The mass of a pen is closest to
A 10 grams.
B 400 grams.
C 4 kilograms.
D 40 kilograms. ✓

3 A rectangle is drawn on a grid. What is the distance around the outside of the rectangle?

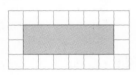

A 6 units
B 8 units
C 12 units
D 16 units ✓

4 Mali ran 3 laps of the 600 metre running track at her local park. What was the total distance she ran?
A 200 metres
B 900 metres
C 1800 metres
D 3600 metres

5 Harold measured his hand-span. It was 20 centimetres long. How many hand-spans would be used to stretch along 1 metre?
A 5
B 10
C 15
D 50 ✓

6 What is the best estimate for the perimeter of this triangle?

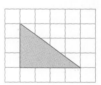

A 8 units
B 10 units
C 12 units
D 18 units

7 The height of *this book* would be closest to
A 8 mm.
B 20 cm. ✓
C 220 cm.
D 4 m.

8 The heights of four dolls are recorded: 42 cm, 57 cm, 44 cm, 39 cm. What is the difference between the tallest and the shortest doll?
A 15 cm
B 18 cm
C 22 cm
D 29 cm

---

9 Which of the following would have a mass that could be measured in tonnes?
A truck
B dog ✓
C egg
D frying pans

10

The sketch shows a balance. This means that 1 cylinder is the same mass as

A ▢
B ▢▢ ✓
C ▢▢▢
D ▢▢▢▢

11 Brian measured the masses of four pumpkins. Which is the lightest pumpkin?
A 650 grams
B 1.2 kg
C 940 grams
D 399 grams ✓

12 Jack and Jill stood on a set of scales and their combined mass was 62 kg. When Jack stood on the scales by himself his mass was 38 kg. What was Jill's mass?
A 24 kg   B 28 kg   C 36 kg   D 100 kg

13 Mary opened a 1 litre carton of custard and poured out 320 mL into a jug. How much custard remains in the carton?

Custard 1 L

A 580 mL
B 680 mL ✓
C 780 mL
D 1320 mL

14 Kerry measures the height of his tomato plant. The plant is 1 metre 50 centimetres. What is this height in centimetres?
A 1 centimetre
B 15 centimetres
C 150 centimetres
D 105 centimetres

15 Andrew's petrol gauge is showing half-full. To fill the petrol tank, he pumps 30 litres into the tank How much petrol is in the tank when it is full?
A 15 litres
B 30 litres
C 45 litres
D 60 litres

16 Each cup contains exactly half a litre. How many cups are needed to hold 2 litres?
A 2
B 4 ✓
C 6
D 8

☞ **Answers and explanations on page 142**

Test Your Skills

MEASUREMENT AND GEOMETRY
Area and volume

20 MIN

1 How many blocks are there on this section of a path?

A 11   B 16   C 21   **D 24** ✓

2 This shape is made up of 1 m squares.

What is its area in square metres?

A 6   **B 7**   C 8   D 9 ✓

3 This is part of a brick wall.

How many bricks will be required for a wall the same length but four rows of bricks high? ✓

A 16   **B 18**   C 20   D 19

4 This open box has sides of 4 cm.

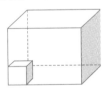

Jack has to fill this box with centicubes. ✓
How many centicubes will he need?

A 16   B 24   C 48   **D 64**

5 Which shape has the greatest area?

A 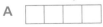   B

C 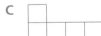   **D** 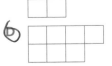 ✓

6 Which playing space would have the largest area?
A a golf course
B a soccer field ✓
C a basketball court
D a tennis court

7 Using the numbers 1, 2, 3 and 4, list these objects from the smallest to the largest (the least volume to the greatest volume).
4 a blown-up party balloon
1 a cherry
2 a ping-pong (table tennis) ball
3 a cricket ball ✓

8 This is a diagram of a tiled area. All the tiles are the same size. How many green tiles were used to tile the area?

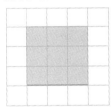

✓

A 4   B 6   **C 9**   D 12

9 Using the numbers 1, 2, 3 and 4, list these objects from the one with the smallest surface area to the one with the greatest surface area.
4 a tablecloth ✓
3 a road STOP sign
1 a bus ticket
2 the title page of a paperback book

10 How many one-centimetre blocks are there in this stack? ✓
A 15
B 16
C 18
D 21

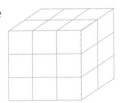

☞ **Explanations on pages 142-143**

MEASUREMENT AND GEOMETRY
Area and volume

❶ Revise your **metric facts** (see Length, mass and capacity, Key Point 1, page 49).

❷ **Area** is the amount of surface of a face or 2D shape.
Area is recorded as square units.
The area of a 5 unit square is 25 square units.
There are four sides, each 5 units long. You can multiply the length of a side by itself to find the area, or count the squares:

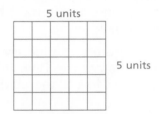

5 × 5 = 25 square units

The area of a **rectangle** 6 units × 3 units is 18 square units. The area is found by multiplying the length by the width, or by counting the squares:

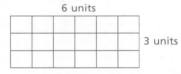

6 × 3 = 18 square units

❸ **Volume** is the space inside a container or the amount of space an object takes up. Volume is recorded as cubic units and we can often count the small cubes that make up a larger solid.

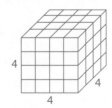

Volume = 4 × 4 × 4
    = 64 cubic units

❹ **Estimating** is an important measurement skill. Know the measurements of some common objects (e.g. a one-litre carton of milk has a mass of about 1 kg).

❺ **All 2D shapes**, including the faces of 3D shapes, have area. Curved surfaces also have area.
All 3D shapes have volume, including 3D shapes with curved surfaces.

❻ **Scale drawings** of **3D shapes** and **objects** can show a reduction or an enlargement. This child's football is drawn to scale. A real football is much larger.

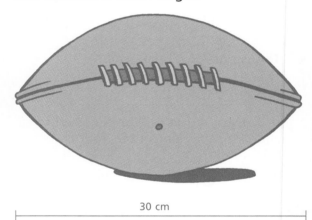

30 cm

❼ You should be able to **convert** (change) between the **basic forms of measurement**.
Example: To convert metres to centimetres, multiply by 100: 2 m = 200 cm
Example: To convert millimetres to centimetres, divide by 10: 150 mm = 15 cm

MEASUREMENT AND GEOMETRY
Area and volume

1 The diagram shows a grid containing a shaded rectangle. What is the area of the rectangle?

A 6 square units   Ⓑ 8 square units
C 10 square units   D 12 square units

2 Which shape has the largest area?

A   Ⓑ

C   D

3 Each square has an area of 20 square metres. How many squares are needed to cover an area of 120 square metres?

20

A 6   Ⓑ 10
C 20   D 100

4 Jannah has drawn triangles and squares, so that 2 triangles have the same area as each square.

How many triangles cover 6 squares?
A 2   B 3   C 6   Ⓓ 12

5 Which would have the greatest area?
A a slice of cheese
B a table
Ⓒ a football field
D a 10 cent coin

6
How many square units are there in the shape?
Ⓐ 10   B 12   C 16   D 20

7 The total area of this shape is 18 square units. How many rows of squares are there in the shape?
A 2   B 3   Ⓒ 4   D 5

8 A carton holds 9 boxes. How many boxes are contained in 6 cartons?
A 3   B 15   Ⓒ 36   Ⓓ 54

9 Which object has the smallest volume?
A golf ball   B basketball
Ⓒ marble   D tennis ball

10 The grid is to be completely covered with stickers. How many more stickers are needed?

21 stickers

11 What is the volume of this solid?

Ⓐ 6 cubic units   B 7 cubic units
C 8 cubic units   D 9 cubic units

The diagram shows a grid containing three shaded shapes.
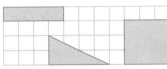

12 What is the area of the rectangle?
A 4 square units   B 6 square units
C 10 square units   Ⓓ 12 square units

13 What is the area of the square? Write your answer in the box: [12] square units

14 What is an estimate for the area of the triangle?
A 4 square units   Ⓑ 8 square units
C 10 square units   D 12 square units

15 Three identical cubes each have a volume of 12 cubic centimetres. When they are glued together, what is the volume of the new shape?
A 15 cubic centimetres
B 24 cubic centimetres
Ⓒ 36 cubic centimetres
D 39 cubic centimetres

16 Kahli wants half the squares shaded. How many more squares need to be shaded?

Ⓐ 1   B 2   C 3   D 4

☞ **Answers and explanations on pages 143-144**

SPELLING
'ie' and 'ei' words and the suffix 'ful'

 With most spelling rules there are exceptions. English words have many different origins (e.g. 'ransack' comes from Norway and 'thug' comes from India).

Key Points

Even though you may not come into contact with some of these words until later in your schooling, it is helpful to know the common 'ie' and 'ei' words that cause problems for students.

1 a In **'ie' and 'ei' words**, the 'i' usually comes before 'e' when the sound is 'ee'.
   Examples: piece, niece, field, yield
   Some exceptions: ceiling, conceit, seize
   b In words where the sound is *not* 'ee', the 'e' usually comes before 'i'.
   Examples: height, their
   c In words where the sound is 'ay', the spelling is usually 'ei'.
   Examples: neighbour, eight, eighty, freight, weight, reign, rein

2 a The **suffix 'ful'** means 'full' but is spelt with only one 'l'.
   Examples: full of care → careful, full of joy → joyful, full of colour → colourful
   b If the word ends with a consonant + y then the 'y' is changed to 'i' before adding 'ful'.
   Examples: beauty → beautiful, mercy → merciful

3 Some **troublesome words** that **sound similar** but have **different spellings** can cause confusion.
   Examples: their (ownership) *and* there (place)
   where (place) *and* wear (clothes) *and* were
   to *and* too (also) *and* two (number).

Test Your Skills

Learn the words below. A common method of learning and self-testing is the **LOOK, SAY, COVER, WRITE, CHECK** method. If you make any mistakes, you should rewrite the word three times correctly, immediately. This is so you will become familiar with the correct spelling. If the word is especially difficult, rewrite it several more times or keep a list of words that you can check regularly.

This week's theme words: 'ie/ei' and 'ful' words in SPORT

playful	_____	skier	_____
hopeful	_____	height	_____
field	_____	zero	_____
tie	_____	tries	_____
skilful	_____	harmful	_____
chief	_____	diet	_____
their	_____	careful	_____
quiet	_____	friend	_____
reins	_____	painful	_____
helpful	_____	brief	_____

Write any troublesome words three times: _____ _____ _____
_____ _____ _____

Real Test

1 The spelling mistakes in these sentences have been highlighted.
Write the correct spelling for each highlighted word in the box.

a   I was still hungery after breakfast.

b   Are you sure you need a holerday?

c   Billy cort the ball then dropped it!

d   Jason hit the ball down the senter of the court.

e   My tomato plant dired during the dry summer.

f   It's your monny so you can spend it.

g   Seven ladys have been invited to play.

h   Sally was sorey after shouting at the umpire.

2 The spelling mistakes in these labels have been highlighted.
Write the correct spelling for each highlighted word in the box.

a   mane door

b   glass panle

c   adress number

16

d   door nob

3 Read the text *Dinosaurs*.
Each line has a word that is incorrect. Write the correct spelling of the word in the box.

Dinosaurs

a   Dinosaur boans have been found in several

b   strainge places. In Queensland a full skeleton

c   was only found arfter a cattle yard had been

d   bilt around it. The cattle trampled the grass

e   to reveal an odd pile off rocks in the middle.

f   Farmers found that they were form a dinosaur.

☞ Answers on page 144

GRAMMAR AND PUNCTUATION
Commas, verbs, tense and 'agreement'

Key Points

1 a **Verbs** are often called **doing words** or **action words**. 'Doing' verbs include verbs for performing actions, thinking and speaking.
Examples: said, swam, collect, study, think, prepare, eat, play

b There is a small group of verbs that are not doing or action words. These are often called **having** or **being** verbs. They do not involve actions or behaviour.
Examples: is, are, am, was, were

c Sometimes these two kinds of verbs are combined to make **two-word verbs**.
Examples: was swimming, am eating, will write

2 a Verbs can tell us when an action *is* happening, *has* happened or *will* happen in the future. This is called **tense**. Tense can be **past**, **present** or **future**. The tense can change the form of the verb.
Examples: I <u>fixed</u> the car. I <u>am fixing</u> the car now. I <u>will fix</u> the car soon.

b Some verbs change when the tense changes.
Examples: ate, eating, will eat; wrote, writing, will write

3 The **subject of a sentence** (what the sentence is about) must always **'agree' with its verb**. (In the examples below, the subject is <u><u>double-underlined</u></u> and the verb is <u>single-underlined</u>.)
Examples: The <u><u>boy</u></u> <u>goes</u> to bed early. The <u><u>boys</u></u> <u>go</u> to bed early.
    The <u><u>star</u></u> <u>was</u> shining brightly. The <u><u>stars</u></u> <u>were</u> shining brightly.

4 When we list things in a sentence, we separate items in the list with a **comma** (,) except for the last two items which are separated by and (and sometimes or).
Examples: At the show I saw cows, horses, sheep **and** dogs.
    Elms, oaks, gums **and** cedars are grown in Australia.

Test Your Skills

1 Underline the three verbs in this passage.
Jan has a new hat. She bought it at a sale. She was looking for a new pair of shoes!

2 Write the tense for each of these sentences (past, present or future).

a I will call my mother later. _____

b Dad built a new kennel for Scruffy. _____

c Mum is putting your dinner on the table! _____

3 Write the correct verb in the spaces

a Mrs Leong _____ carefully past the school. (drive, drives)

b My friends _____ watching television when I arrived. (was, were)

c An engine _____ us each morning about six o'clock. (wake, wakes)

4 Write the number of commas needed in these sentences.

a Under the house there were ants spiders sandflies and mosquitoes. _____

b Red blue green indigo and yellow are some of the rainbow's colours. _____

c The coach decided that only Tanya Jane or Fay could carry the flag. _____

Answers: **1** has, bought, was looking **2 a** future **b** past **c** present **3 a** drives **b** were **c** wakes **4 a** two **b** three **c** one

GRAMMAR AND PUNCTUATION
Commas, verbs, tense and 'agreement'

❶ Which of the following correctly completes this sentence?

The twins _____ in my team last year.

is	are	were	was
A	B	C	D

❷ Which of the following correctly completes this sentence?

We have a new car. It is _____ orange sports car in the shed.

a	the	an	and
A	B	C	D

❸ Which of the following correctly completes this sentence?

We _____ the new car later in the morning.

cleaned	cleaning	will clean	clean
A	B	C	D

❹ Which word in the following sentence is a verb?
Bruce has a good idea for the Christmas concert.

has	good	idea	concert
A	B	C	D

❺ Which of the following correctly completes this sentence?

The baby crawled _____ the table to get the spoon she had dropped.

down	up	into	under
A	B	C	D

❻ Which of the following correctly completes this sentence?

After we had _____ by the gate we were spotted in the lane!

crept	creep	creped	creeped
A	B	C	D

❼ How many commas should be used in this sentence?
Martin invited Jake Leo Mark and Graham to his party.

none	one	two	three
A	B	C	D

Read the text *The Circus*. The text has some gaps. Choose the best option to fill each gap.

The Circus
The circus was in town.

Dad let me go with _____ Jack and

❽
uncle	Uncle	uncle,	Uncle,
A	B	C	D

_____ family. There was his wife and

❾
hes	he's	his'	his
A	B	C	D

_____ four children, Meg, Lenny,

❿
Their	their	there	There
A	B	C	D

☞ **Answers and explanations on page 144**

_____ and Justine. They all go to school

11

Perry,	perry,	Perry	Perry.
A	B	C	D

except Justine _____ is still a baby. Are

12

that	which	what	who
A	B	C	D

babies too young for the _____

13

circus?	Circus?	circus.	circus!
A	B	C	D

14 Choose the word that is not required in this sentence.
A branch fell down from the tree during the squall last night.

fell	down	during	squall
A	B	C	D

15 Which sentence has the correct punctuation?
  A This can't be the way to the park, or the school.
  B This cant be the way to the park or the school?
  C This can't be the way to the park or the school.
  D This cant be the way to the park or the school.

16 Which of the following correctly completes the sentence?

Lester's injury is _____ than it was last night.

worse	worser	more worse	worst
A	B	C	D

17 Shade a bubble to show where the missing comma (,) should go.

Later in the day ⬩ we played cricket ⬩ volley ball ⬩ and had a game ⬩ of rounders.
       (A)   (B)   (C)   (D)

18 Which sentence has the correct punctuation?
  A Will we put oranges apples, or lemons in the basket?
  B Will we put, oranges, apples, or lemons, in the basket?
  C Will we put oranges, apples or lemons, in the basket?
  D Will we put oranges, apples or lemons in the basket?

☞ **Answers and explanations on page 144**

Test Your Skills

READING
Understanding recounts

A recount is a record of events that happened in sequence. Recounts have several forms. They can be personal or historical. They may also contain opinions or personal comments of the events. A diary is a form of recount. Many newspaper articles are recounts.

Read this extract from *My Diary* by Jenny Jarman-Walker and answer the questions. Circle the correct answer.

Monday 10th April

Dear Diary

I am writing this in the taxi on the way to the TV studio. It's 6:45 in the morning and it's just getting light. It was dark and cold when the alarm went off, and I wanted to stay in bed a bit longer. Mum said, 'No.'

Mr Davis is driving me this morning. He doesn't talk much, which is good. I can write more. I can see the grass on the side of the road. It's still wet. I suppose it will be sunny later on. Let's hope so. I hate it when filming stops because of rain.

My 'call' is for 7:30. Before we finish work every day we are all given a call sheet. It has all the information about what we'll be doing the next day, which scenes we'll be filming (or 'shooting' as they say), and what time everyone has to be at work. Under my name is 'Call time 7:30 a.m.', and Scenes 4, 5 and 7.

Hey, we're here already. I'll run out of the taxi as fast as I can and into the studio so I can stay warm.

It's 8:30 and I have changed into my wardrobe for the day. I know 'wardrobe' sounds funny as if I should have knobs or handles, but that's what they call what I'm wearing today.

Penny

---

1 What work does Penny do?
 A taxi-driving B writing C acting D shooting

2 What is the most likely reason Penny wanted to stay in bed?
 A to keep warm B she was tired
 C the alarm went off early D she hadn't been 'called'

3 Penny was glad that Mr Davis wasn't talking because she wanted to
 A sleep. B learn lines. C write. D get changed.

4 In the passage, the word 'shooting' refers to
 A working. B hunting. C dressing. D filming.

5 When does Penny get her 'call sheet'?
 A at 7:30 each morning B at the end of each day
 C before she leaves for the studio D as soon as she gets to the studio

6 Write the numbers 1, 2, 3, and 4 in the boxes to show the order in which Penny does things.

 begins writing starts a taxi ride puts on her 'wardrobe' hears her alarm

READING
Understanding recounts

Read the passage from *Before Computers* by Bill Barry and answer the questions. Circle the correct answer.

Many thousands of years ago writing had not been <u>invented</u>. People recorded numbers by scratching marks on trees, stones and the ground.

They first made these marks to record the passing of time, like days, new moons and the seasons. Hunters made marks to keep a tally of the animals they caught.

The word 'score' in sport and games comes from numbers 'scored' (that means scratched) on wood.

The first numbers were just scratch marks. They looked like this: (|) | } | / | (|

Over hundreds of years these 'numbers' changed in different ways in different countries.

Now, most of the world's numbers look like this: `0 1 2 3 4 5 6 7 8 9`

The numbers we use on bank cheques look quite different: `0 1 2 3 4 5 6 7 8 9`

The numbers on digital watches and calculators look different again: `0 1 2 3 4 5 9 7 8 9`

Maybe numbers will change more in the future. Who knows?

---

1 What is the main idea in the extract?
   A People are smarter today than they were hundreds of years ago.
   B Tallies cannot be used to show the passing of time.
   C People could write before they could use numbers.
   D The numbers we use have changed over a long period of time.

2 What is a tally mark most like?
   A an alphabet letter   B a digital number   C a line   D a score card

3 You would be most likely to find a number written like this **4** on a
   A cheque.   B digital watch.   C cave wall.   D bank note.

4 Which phrase best completes this sentence?
Nowadays, most numbers used across the world look ____? ____ .
   A much the same   B like digital numbers
   C like tally marks   D very different

5 Which word could best replace 'invented' in the passage?
   A produced   B found   C created   D solved

6 Select the best title for this extract.
   A Understanding How Cheques Work   B Caring for Your Calculator
   C Telling the Time with a Digital Watch   D How Numbers Continue to Change

☞ **Answers and explanations on page 145**

Test Your Skills

7 MIN

The purpose of an explanation is to tell how or why something happens. Explanations can be about natural or scientific events, how things work or things that happen. Illustrations are often provided to make information easier to understand.

Study this information on Great Dinosaurs and answer the questions. Circle the correct answer.

Ankylosaurus (fused lizard)

Pronounced: An-key-low-saw-rus
Length: 10–11 metres
Height: 3–4 metres
Mass: 3–4 tonnes
Habitat: Bushland and plains
Location: North America

Triceratops (three-horned face)

Pronounced: Try-serr-a-tops
Length: 7–9 metres
Height: 10–11 metres
Mass: 5–6 tonnes
Habitat: Bushland and plains
Location: North America

Tyrannosaurus (tyrant lizard)

Pronounced: Tie-ran-o-saw-rus
Length: Over 12 metres
Height: 10–11 metres
Mass: 6–7 tonnes
Habitat: Plains
Location: Asia and North America

Brachiosaurus (arm lizard)

Pronounced: Brack-ee-o-saw-rus
Length: Up to 27 metres
Height: 12 metres or more
Mass: 50–100 tonnes
Habitat: Forests near lakes
Location: North America and Africa

❶ Which word, with a similar meaning, could best replace 'habitat'?
A environment   B plains   C setting   D neighbourhood

❷ Which of the dinosaurs shown above weighed the least amount?
A Ankylosaurus   B Triceratops   C Tyrannosaurus   D Brachiosaurus

❸ Which of the dinosaurs shown above lived near lakes?
A Ankylosaurus   B Triceratops   C Tyrannosaurus   D Brachiosaurus

❹ Which of the dinosaurs shown above lived in Asia?
A Ankylosaurus   B Triceratops   C Tyrannosaurus   D Brachiosaurus

❺ In each diagram is an illustration of a person. This is to show
A what the dinosaurs ate.   B how large the dinosaurs were.
C how dangerous the dinosaurs could be.   D how scientists study the dinosaurs.

❻ This information would be most likely found in a
A manual.   B novel.   C diary.   D reference book.

Answers: 1 A 2 A 3 D 4 C 5 B 6 D

☞ **Explanations on pages 145-146**

Real Test

READING
Understanding explanations

Read the extract from *Pandas* by Christine Deacon and answer the questions. Circle the correct answer.

Pandas are in danger of becoming extinct. In 1977 there were only 1000 giant pandas left in the wild in China. Why are they dying out?

Pandas have few natural enemies. Black leopards and wild dogs will take baby pandas if the mother is not careful.

But the panda's natural enemies are not the problem.

Giant pandas are very <u>timid</u> animals. They will give up their territory if humans settle close by. Some of their natural habitat has been cleared for farming and forestry, taking away dense forests that pandas need to live in.

Another problem is caused by bamboo dieback. Bamboos only flower every forty years and afterwards the plants die back. This means that there is not enough food for the panda, and many of them die.

When the number of pandas in each isolated area becomes very low, the next generation suffers too. This is because there may not be enough animals of the right sex and age in the same area, so that pandas cannot find a suitable mate.

1 The purpose of the extract is to
   A inform readers of the feeding habits of pandas.
   B explain why pandas are in danger of dying out.
   C show ways of getting more food for pandas.
   D encourage people to protect pandas from wild dogs.

2 Which title best suits the extract?
   A Natural Enemies   B Panda Problems   C Bamboo Dieback   D Baby Pandas

3 Which of the following is **not** a threat to young pandas?
   A leopards   B food shortage   C farming   D global warming

4 What do pandas do when humans start living close by? The pandas
   A move away.   B become dangerous. C attack the people. D eat their plants.

5 The word 'timid' could best replaced with which word?
   A tired   B tragic   C shy   D frightened

6 How often does bamboo get flowers?
   A never   B every forty years C yearly   D all the time

7 What is meant when an animal is described as 'extinct'?
   A There are not many left in the wild.   B The only animals of that type are in zoos.
   C That animal lives in isolated areas.   D There are no living animals of that type.

☞ **Answers and explanations on page 146**

Real Test

READING
Understanding explanations

Read the extract from *Hearty Facts* by Shane Power and answer the questions.

Your heart is a mighty machine. It is so busy that it needs every bit of help from its owner—you. Heart attacks mostly occur in middle-aged people, but the damage in your arteries can begin in childhood. That is why it is important to take care of your heart while you are young. To reduce your risk of heart disease:

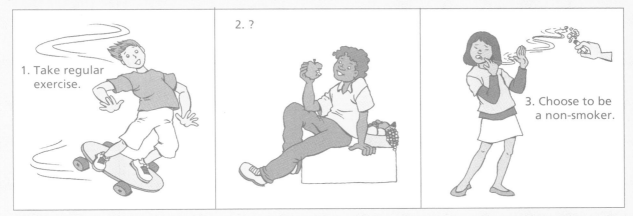

1. Take regular exercise.

2. ?

3. Choose to be a non-smoker.

The way you live now and the choices you make now and in the future are an important part of keeping your heart healthy—or unhealthy.

1 Who is most likely to have a heart attack? Write your answer on the line.

_____

2 The pictures from the extract contain advice on how to care for your heart. The second caption has been removed. What would be a suitable caption?
A   Sit down more often.
B   Eat healthy foods.
C   Don't work too hard.
D   Eat snacks between meals.

3 Who does the extract say is most responsible for a the health of a person's heart?
A   its owner
B   the person's parents
C   the family doctor
D   a sports coach

4 What are arteries?
A   pictures in a first aid manual
B   a name for the parts of the heart
C   places where artworks are kept
D   tubes in the body that carry blood

5 The word *regular* could best be replaced with
A   frequent.
B   reasonable.
C   weekly.
D   gentle.

6 Why is the heart called a mighty machine?
A   The heart is very large.
B   We die when it doesn't work.
C   It pumps without stopping for a lifetime.
D   It is red like a fire engine.

7 This extract is most likely part of
A   a story.
B   a myth or legend.
C   a report.
D   an explanation.

☞ Answers and explanations on page 146

TIPS FOR WRITING NARRATIVE TEXTS

A **narrative** is a form of prose writing that tells a story. Its main purpose is to entertain. Writers of narratives create experiences that are shared with the reader. To do this the writer uses literary techniques. Such techniques include figurative language (similes, metaphors, alliteration, onomatopoeia, rhetorical questions and repetition), variety in sentence length and type, variety in paragraph length, and direct speech.

In any narratives, the author is the person who wrote the story. The narrator is the person (*I*) who is both in the story and who tells the story.

When writing narratives it is best to keep the following points in mind. They will help you get the best possible mark.

Before you start writing

- Read the question and check the stimulus material carefully. *Stimulus material* means the topic, title, picture, words, phrases or extract of writing you are given to base your writing on.
- Write about something you know. Don't try to write about something way outside your experience.
- Decide if you are going to be writing in the first person (you become a character in your story) or in the third person (about other characters). When writing in the first person be careful not to overuse the pronoun *I* (e.g. *I did this, I did that*).
- Take a few moments to jot your ideas down on a piece of paper. Write down the order in which things happen. These could be the points in your story where you start new paragraphs.
- Remember: stories have a beginning, middle and end. It sounds simple but many stories fail because one of these three parts is not well written.

The introduction

- Don't start with *Once upon a time*—this is too clichéd and predictable.
- Don't tell the reader too much in the beginning. Make the reader want to read on to find out more. The beginning should introduce a problem to be solved.

The body

- **In the middle of your story include events that make solving the problem more difficult or doubtful.** This makes the story interesting.
- **Use a setting that you are familiar with**, e.g. home, school, sport, holiday place or shopping centre. You will then be able to describe the setting realistically.
- **Choose characters that are like people you know** because they are easier to imagine. You don't have to use their real names—it's probably best not to!
- **Use your imagination to make the story more interesting**, but don't try to fill it with weird or disgusting events.
- **Enhance your story with the use of literary techniques**, e.g. similes, metaphors, onomatopoeia and alliteration.
- **Make your paragraphing work for you**. New paragraphs are usually needed for new incidents in your story, changes in time or place, descriptions that move from one sense to another, or changes in the character who is speaking.

The conclusion

- The ending is the hardest part to write because it has to have something to do with the beginning.
- Never end your stories with: *and it was just a dream; I was saved by a superhero (or by magic); I was dead; and they lived happily ever after!* Endings like these just tell the marker that you don't have a creative way to end your story.

When you have finished writing give yourself a few minutes to read through your story. Now is the time to check spelling and punctuation, and to insert words that have been accidentally left out.

Real Test and Tips

There is no way of knowing for certain what type of writing will be included in NAPLAN tests in years to come. This is an opportunity for you to practise different types of writing.

Before you start, read the General writing tips on pages 20–21 and the Tips for writing narrative texts on page 66.

Today you are going to write a narrative or story. Look at the picture on the right. The idea for your story is an alien. It could be a lost alien or a lonely alien. The story could be about you and the alien or about other people and the alien.

Think about where your story takes place. It could be at home, at school, or even at a cinema or shopping centre! You could add a description of the alien and tell about its behaviour. Think about when your story takes place: daytime or night-time, summer or winter. Your story might be amusing or it might be serious. Think about how the people in your story react.

Before you start writing, give some thought to:
- where your story takes place
- the characters and what they do in your story
- the events that take place in your story and the problems that have to be resolved
- how your story begins, what happens in your story, and how your story ends.

Don't forget to:
- plan your story before you start writing
- write in correctly formed sentences and take care with paragraphing.
- choose your words carefully and pay attention to your spelling and punctuation
- write neatly but don't waste time
- quickly check your story once you have finished.

Start writing here.

_____

_____

_____

_____

_____

_____

_____

_____

_____

☞ **Marking guide on pages 146-147**

Real Test and Tips

There is no way of knowing for certain what type of writing will be included in NAPLAN tests in years to come. This is an opportunity for you to practise different types of writing.
Before you start, read the General writing tips on pages 20–21 and the Tips for writing narrative texts on page 66.

Today you are going to write a narrative or story. The idea for your story is A SURPRISE VISITOR.

Think about all of the places where a visitor might unexpectedly turn up. It could be at home but it could be at school, or a party, or at a sporting match. Who is the visitor? Why did the visitor suddenly arrive? Maybe the visitor is an animal. Your story could be about your experiences or different people in situations where they are faced with a surprise visitor. Think about the way people react in your story. Think about when your story takes place – daytime or night time, weekends or weekdays or while on holidays. Your story might be amusing or it might be serious.

Before you start writing, give some thought to:
- where your story takes place
- the characters and what they do in your story
- the events that take place in your story and the problems that have to be resolved
- how your story begins, what happens in your story, and how your story ends.

Don't forget to:
- plan your story before you start writing
- write in correctly formed sentences and take care with paragraphing.
- choose your words carefully and pay attention to your spelling and punctuation
- write neatly but don't waste time
- quickly check your story once you have finished.

Start writing here.

_____

_____

_____

_____

_____

_____

_____

☞ **Marking guide on pages 147-148**

Only one week to go!

Week 4

This is what we cover this week:

Day 1 **Number and Algebra/**
Statistics and Probability: ◎ Patterns, algebra, chance and probability
Statistics and Probability: ◎ Graphs, tables and data

Day 2 **Spelling:** ◎ Words ending in 'y', homophones, days of the week and 'demon' words
◎ Common misspellings
Grammar and Punctuation: ◎ Adverbs, prepositions, pronouns and apostrophes

Day 3 **Reading:** ◎ Following procedures
◎ Interpreting other texts

Day 4 **Writing:** ◎ Description of a place or scene
◎ Description of a person
◎ Explanation

Test Your Skills

NUMBER AND ALGEBRA/ STATISTICS AND PROBABILITY
Patterns, algebra, chance and probability

20 min

Circle the correct answer.

PATTERNS AND ALGEBRA

1 $6 \times 4 = 2 \times \square$

$\square = ?$

A 8   B 10   C 12   D 24

2 Which pattern is an example of adding 2?

A 3, 6, 12, 24, 48   B 2, 4, 6, 8, 10, 12
C 2, 3, 4, 5, 6, 7   D 14, 12, 10, 8, 6, 4

3 If $18 \div 9 = 2$, then $9 \times \square = 18$.

$\square = ?$

A 2   B 9   C 11   D 20

4 This is the start of a number pattern.

3, 4, 6, 9, ...

If the pattern is continued, what will be the fifth term?

A 10   B 11   C 12   D 13

5 $6 + 5 - \square = 9$

$\square = ?$

A 2   B 11   C 12   D 31

6 $15 + 15 + 15 + 15 = \square \times 4$

$\square = ?$

A 15   B 19   C 29   D 58

7 Find the missing number in this number pattern.

5	6	8	10	13
9	10	12	14	?

A 15   B 16   C 17   D 18

8 Here is a series of stars.

★ ★ ★ ★ ★ ★ ★ ★
★ ★ ★ ★ ★ ★
★ ★ ★ ★
★ ★
???

How many stars should replace the question marks?

A 0   B 1   C 2   D 4

CHANCE AND PROBABILITY

1 If a die is tossed once, what is the chance of throwing a 4?

A 1 chance in 2   B 1 chance in 4
C 1 chance in 5   D 1 chance in 6

2 Which term best describes the possibility of cold days in winter?

A unlikely   B most likely
C not likely   D certain

3 Tim has 4 red blocks and 4 green blocks in a bag. Without looking he removes one. What is the chance it is a red block?

A 1 in 2   B 1 in 4
C 1 in 8   D 1 in 16

4 How many three-digit numbers can be made with 6, 9 and 4?

A 3   B 6   C 9   D 19

5 Myra made this spinner. She painted it these colours.

What colour is Myra most likely to get when she spins her spinner?

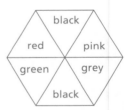

A red   B pink
C green   D black

6 3K conducted a survey of large vehicles passing their school in one hour. These were their results.

Vehicle	Number
Bus	3
Truck	12
Van	17
Utility	8

The next vehicle to go past is most likely to be a

A bus.   B truck.   C van.   D utility.

☞ **Explanations on page 148**

Key Points

NUMBER AND ALGEBRA/ STATISTICS AND PROBABILITY
Patterns, algebra, chance and probability

PATTERNS AND ALGEBRA

1 **Relating addition to subtraction:**
The total of two (or more) numbers produces a number of facts.

Example: 5 + 6 = 11, 6 + 5 = 11, 11 − 5 = 6,
11 − 6 = 5

2 **Relating multiplication to division:**
The product of two (or more) numbers produces a number of facts.

Example: 2 × 4 = 8, 4 × 2 = 8, 8 ÷ 2 = 4,
8 ÷ 4 = 2

3 Patterns may be based on **shapes**. For example:

◆ ◆ ◆ ● ● ◆ ◆ ● ● ◆ ◆ ● ?

The next shape in the pattern will be ●.

4 **Multiplication is repeated addition:**

8 + 8 + 8 + 8 + 8 = 5 × 8 because there are five lots of eight to be added.

5 **Number sequences** can be made up of increasing numbers (e.g. 2, 4, 6, 8, ...) or decreasing numbers (e.g. 9, 7, 5, ...). Sequences can be devised on all four operations (+, −, ×, ÷).

6 **More difficult sequences** may involve two or more steps. In the following sequence, you multiply the first number by 2, then add 1 to the second number, etc.
5, 10, 11, 22, 23, ...
The next number will be 46.

7 You should be able to **find the missing number in a number sentence**.

Examples:
6 + ? = 13
The missing number is 7.
The missing number can be in any position.

Example:
□ ÷ 3 = 8 − 3
Then □ = 15 (15 ÷ 3 = 5 and 8 − 3 = 5)

8 The signs + and − are called '**weak signs**'. The signs × and ÷ are called '**strong signs**'.

In any calculation with mixed signs the strong signs are calculated first.

To calculate 6 + 4 × 2, first multiply 4 × 2 and then add 6 to the total, so that 6 + 8 = 14.

9 In **number patterns** you are asked to find a number after you have been given a set of examples.

1	6	8	11	13
2	7	9	12	?

In this pattern, the missing number is 14. Each number in the lower row is one greater than the number directly above it.

CHANCE AND PROBABILITY

1 **Chance** refers to the possibility of an event occurring and can be expressed in numerical terms (e.g. 1 chance in 3). **Probability** also refers to the possibility of an event occurring.

2 The **probability of an event** occurring can be placed on a scale of 0 (zero) to 1 (one).

```
  0                                    1
impossible                         certain
```

For example, the probability of a person living for 100 years would be closer to 0 than 1 on this scale.

3 **Some common objects** used in **games of chance** are dice (singular: die), coins, spinners, playing cards and chocolate wheels.

4 The **chance of tossing a head** with a coin is 1 chance in 2, or $\frac{1}{2}$, or 50%.

The chance of getting a six with the roll of a die is 1 chance in 6, or $\frac{1}{6}$, or about 16%.

NUMBER AND ALGEBRA/ STATISTICS AND PROBABILITY
Patterns, algebra, chance and probability

5 **Arrangements** refer to all possible groupings of a group of objects.

Example:

How many arrangements are there for the letters A, B, and C?

The arrangements are ABC, ACB, BAC, BCA, CAB and CBA. There are six arrangements.

6 From **data (information) gained**, the likelihood of an event happening can be predicted. Weather records allow scientists to predict what the weather will be like at a particular time of the year.

7 **Surveys** are often used to collect data. This was the result of a survey of pets that students in four classes have at home.

Class	Cats	Dogs
2A	8	2
3C	12	5
4A	9	8
5F	11	4

Therefore it is **most likely** that another class surveyed will have more cats than dogs.

8 Here are **some words** you should be familiar with in **chance and probability**:

- possible/impossible
- certain/uncertain
- likely/unlikely
- probable
- likelihood.

Real Test

NUMBER AND ALGEBRA/ STATISTICS AND PROBABILITY
Patterns, algebra, chance and probability

1 The pattern is made by adding 13 to each number:

11   24   37 ____

What is the next number?

A   40   B   50
C   51   D   60

2 **11   27   32   42   46**
Jasmine chooses two numbers from the list and finds that the difference between them is 14. Which two numbers did she choose?

A   11 and 32   B   27 and 42
C   27 and 46   D   32 and 46

3 12 + 12 + 12 + 12 + 12 = ☐ × 12

Write the correct answer in the square.

4 Complete the pattern:

85   77   69   61 ☐

A   8   B   52
C   53   D   55

5 The same number is written in each circle to make the number sentence correct.

◯ + ◯ + ◯ = 33

What number is placed in the circles?

A   11   B   12   C   15   D   16

6 Melanie coloured squares on this chart in an ascending order. What will be the eighth number shaded?

1	2	3	4	5
6	7	8	9	10
11	12	13	14	15
16	17	18	19	20
21	22	23	24	25

A   18   B   21
C   24   D   25

7

1	2	3	4	5
4	8	12	16	?

What is the missing number in the table?

A   18   B   20   C   22   D   24

8 Which of these shows counting forwards by fives?

A   25   35   45   55   65
B   5   50   500 5000 50 000
C   40   45   50   55   60
D   5   55   555 5555 55 555

9 Complete this pattern: 40 – 16 = 24
                                50 – 16 = 34
                                60 – 16 = 44
                                90 – 16 = ☐

What number is written in the box?

A   45   B   47   C   74   D   84

10    **?**

How many squares are in the next diagram?

A   5   B   10   C   12   D   15

11 Kevin is counting backwards by 6:
   90, 84, 78, 72, …
What is the next number in the pattern?

A   66   B   60   C   56   D   54

12 Jasmin made this spinner and painted it these colours. What colour is she most likely to get on her next spin?

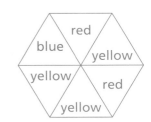

A   red
B   blue
C   yellow   D   pink

13 Yanni rolls a die.
What is the chance she rolls a 4?

A   1 in 6   B   1 in 4
C   1 in 3   D   1 in 8

14 What is the chance that the sun will rise tomorrow?

A   impossible   B   likely
C   possible   D   certain

A bag contains 20 jelly beans. In the bag there are 12 black jelly beans, 3 red jelly beans and the rest are green.

15 How many jelly beans are green?   ☐

16 Without looking, Marcia chooses a jelly bean from the bag. What is the chance that it is red?

A   3 in 12   B   3 in 15
C   3 in 20   D   1 in 3

☞ **Answers and explanations on pages 148-149**

Test Your Skills

STATISTICS AND PROBABILITY
Graphs, tables and data

Circle the correct answer.

1 Here are the scores for a darts competition.

David	23
Joyce	25
Allie	52
Lorenz	23
Melody	11

Which two players got the same scores?

A David and Joyce B David and Lorenz
C Joyce and Allie D Joyce and Lorenz

2 Refer to the table above.

If Melody has another throw, what must she get to have a higher score than Joyce?

A 11   B 13   C 14   D 15

3 Jamie received a gift of $100. This graph shows how he spent his money.

Jamie spent the same amount on fast food as he spent on

A CDs.   B a T-shirt.
C his mobile phone.   D bus fares.

4 This pictograph shows the number of phones on each floor of a factory.

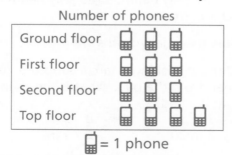

Number of phones

Ground floor	
First floor	
Second floor	
Top floor	

= 1 phone

What is the total number of phones in the factory?

A 4   B 13   C 14   D 26

5 What number does this tally represent?

卌 卌 卌 ||

A 17   B 16   C 15   D 13

6 This graphs shows the sales of family portraits by classes at a school fete.

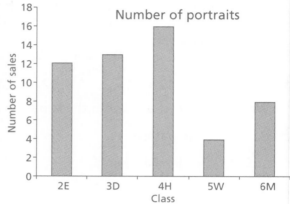

How many portraits did 4H sell?

A 10   B 12   C 14   D 16

7 Refer to the graph above.
How many classes took part in the selling of family portraits?

A 4   B 5   C 6   D 7

8 The results of a survey show the drinks students prefer.

Drink	Boys	Girls
Water	4	7
Juice	8	7
Milk	2	5
Soft drink	8	1

Which drink is most preferred overall?

A water   B milk
C juice   D soft drink

9 Refer to the table above.
How many boys were in the survey?

A 8   B 9   C 20   D 22

☞ **Explanations on page 149**

Answers: 1 B 2 D 3 B 4 B 5 A 6 D 7 B 8 C 9 D

Key Points

STATISTICS AND PROBABILITY
Graphs, tables and data

1 Types of graphs:

a **Bar graphs** can be presented vertically (with the bars going up and down) or horizontally (with the bars going from left to right). Take care with the horizontal and vertical labels.

Distances in long jump

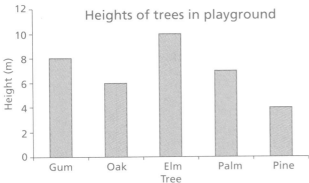

Heights of trees in playground

b **Pie graphs** (or sector graphs) show portions or sections of a whole. This graph shows how Jarrad spent his two hours of homework time.
Jarrad spent half his time doing Maths.

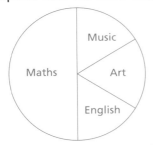

c **Line graphs** show data joined by segments of a line.
On the following graph, the temperature at 2 pm was 25°C.

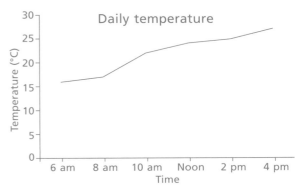

Daily temperature

d **Pictographs** (or picture graphs) use pictures to display data.

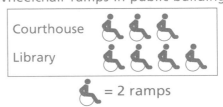

Wheelchair ramps in public buildings

| Courthouse | 🦽 🦽 🦽 |
| Library | 🦽 🦽 🦽 🦽 |

🦽 = 2 ramps

This means that the library had 8 ramps and the courthouse had 6 ramps.
Half pictures tell you half the number:

🦽 = 1 ramp

2 Types of tables:

a **One-way tables**. These show one line of data.

Money saved

Marco	Tony	Bindi	Olivia	Loren
$12	$16	$23	$7	$12

Bindi saved the most money.

b **Two-way tables**. These tables can be read down and across.

Maths marks

	Sue	Joe	Leo	Eve
Test 1	60%	55%	48%	76%
Test 2	60%	53%	58%	78%

Eve's total score was the highest.

3 A **tally** is a quick way to keep a record or a score and add up totals. Tallies are made with four vertical marks and one cross mark equalling five.
Examples: IIII = 5; IIII II = 7

Real Test

STATISTICS AND PROBABILITY
Graphs, tables and data

20 MIN

The school held a pie drive. The sales were recorded in the pictograph:

Yr 3	Yr 4	Yr 5	Yr 6

🥧 = 10 pies

1 How many pies were sold by year 3?
A 4 **B** 10 **C** 40 **D** 100

2 How many year groups sold more than 15 pies?
A 1 **B** 2 **C** 3 **D** 4

3 The school makes a profit of $2 for each pie sold. How much profit will the school make on all the pies sold?
A $100 **B** $200 **C** $1000 **D** $2000

Thirty-six students were surveyed. The table represents their favourite sports.

Soccer	Netball	Swimming	Basketball
6	12	9	?

4 What was their favourite sport?
A basketball **B** soccer
C swimming **D** netball

5 How many of the 36 students surveyed chose basketball?
A 4 **B** 6 **C** 9 **D** 90

The graph shows the way students travelled to the school this morning.

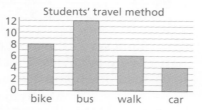

Students' travel method

6 How many students walked to school?
A 6 **B** 12 **C** 18 **D** 28

7 How many students were surveyed?
A 12 **B** 16 **C** 18 **D** 30

8 On the way home from school that day, every student travelled the same way, except for twins Bennie and Bobbie. Instead of catching the bus home, they were driven home in their mother's car.

How many students caught the bus home?
A 8 **B** 10 **C** 18 **D** 28

Suzi recorded the ages of the children at the holiday club in the table below:

Age	7	8	9	10	11	12
Children	4	6	12	8	4	5

9 How many children attended the club?
A 6 **B** 39 **C** 44 **D** 50

10 How many children were aged more than 10 years old?
A 9 **B** 11 **C** 17 **D** 23

The table shows the number of laps Quentin swam over 5 days. The total number of laps Quentin swam over the 5 days was 40 laps.

Mon	Tue	Wed	Thu	Fri
8	6	12		10

11 How many laps did he swim on Thursday?
A 4 **B** 5 **C** 6 **D** 8

12 On how many days did he swim more than 8 laps?
A 1 **B** 2 **C** 3 **D** 4

The table shows the amount of money that four students spent at the canteen:

Bree	Robbi	Tricia	Sandi
$2.90	$0.80	$2.25	$2.05

13 Who spent the most money?
A Bree **B** Robbi
C Tricia **D** Sandi

14 How many students spent at least $2? ☐

15 What is the best estimate for the total amount of money that the students spent?
A $4.00 **B** $8.00
C $12.00 **D** $16.00

16 A survey was held to find the number of pet owners and non-pet owners at a party.

	Pet owner	Non pet
Males	4	11
Females	6	9

How many males were at the party?
A 4 **B** 11 **C** 15 **D** 20

☞ **Answers and explanations on pages 149-150**

**Key Points
and
Test Your
Skills**

SPELLING

*Words ending in 'y', homophones,
days of the week and 'demon' words*

15 min

With most spelling rules there are exceptions. English words have many different origins (e.g. 'plaza' comes from Spain and 'hamburger' comes from Germany).

Key Points

1 **To add a suffix to a word ending with 'y'**, change the 'y' to an 'i' before adding the suffix. Some common suffixes are 'ly', 'ness', 'less', 'est' and 'ful' (see page 56 for 'ful').
Examples: happi<u>ly</u>, lazi<u>ly</u>; happi<u>ness</u>, lazi<u>ness</u>; piti<u>less</u>, penni<u>less</u>; easi<u>est</u>, angri<u>est</u>; beautiful

2 **Homophones** are words that sound the same but have different spellings. You need to be able to use them correctly.
Examples: <u>knew</u> (understood), <u>new</u> (not used); <u>no</u> (disagree), <u>know</u> (understand); <u>where</u> (place), <u>wear</u> (dress); <u>break</u> (smash), <u>brake</u> (slow down); <u>four</u> (4), <u>for</u> (belonging to; use); <u>tail</u> (belonging to an animal), <u>tale</u> (story); <u>right</u> (correct), <u>write</u> (with a pen)

3 The **days of the week are proper nouns**, so they begin with capital letters: Sunday, Monday, Tuesday, Wednesday, Thursday, Friday, Saturday.

4 **'Demon' words** are words that are commonly misspelled. It is important to know the spelling of these words. Here are 25 examples.

almost	can't (cannot)	kitchen	children	half
also	clothes	safety	you're (you are)	halves
they're (they are)	eight	garbage	won't (will not)	forty
write	library	poetry	aunt	answer
writing	science	balloon	using	women

Test Your Skills

Learn the words below. A common method of learning and self-testing is the **LOOK, SAY, COVER, WRITE, CHECK** method. If you make any mistakes, you should rewrite the word three times correctly, immediately. This is so you will become familiar with the correct spelling. If the word is especially difficult, rewrite it several more times or keep a list of words that you can check regularly.

This week's theme words: FICTION

snowman	_____	hero	_____
fairy	_____	heroes	_____
fairies	_____	protect	_____
dragon	_____	story	_____
slay	_____	stories	_____
giant	_____	fearful	_____
ending	_____	cast	_____
prince	_____	casting	_____
knight	_____	forever	_____
witch	_____	happily	_____
castle	_____	forest	_____

Write any troublesome words three times: _____ _____ _____

_____ _____ _____

Real Test

SPELLING
Common misspellings

1 The spelling mistakes in these sentences have been highlighted.
Write the correct spelling for each highlighted word in the box.

a   All at wonce I felt afraid.

b   The baloon burst and we all jumped!

c   Before useing a fork you must wash your hands.

d   My unckle sent me a birthday present.

e   We had freid fish with our chips.

f   David was reddy before his mother.

g   When Val scored a goal we all cheared.

h   We don't have eny water left.

2 The spelling mistakes in these labels have been highlighted.
Write the correct spelling for each highlighted word in the box.

a   hot warter jug

b   plastic couver

c   spourt

d   kittle base

3 Read the text *The Visit*.
Each line has a word that is incorrect. Write the correct spelling in the box.

The Visit

a   They raced off doun the street, with their dog,

b   Spot, runing ahead of them. Soon they reached

c   the front gate of the old house. Sumeone was

d   watching from the winder near the door. Spot

e   darted up to the front door. The boys folowed.

f   It was time to nock and ask their question.

☞ **Answers on pages 150-151**

GRAMMAR AND PUNCTUATION
Adverbs, prepositions, pronouns and apostrophes

Key Points

1 **Pronouns** are words that take the place of nouns.
Example: Josh gave the ball to Katie. <u>He</u> gave it to <u>her</u>. ('He' and 'her' are pronouns.)
Here are some common pronouns: I, we, me, us, you, they, them, he, she, him, her, it.

2 **Prepositions** show the relationship between a noun or pronoun and another word. They show the position of something (pre<u>position</u>). *Examples*: at, in, above, under, off, until, up, upon, beside, between.

3 **Adverbs** help verbs. They add extra meaning to the verbs. They tell how, when or where something happened. Many adverbs end in 'ly'. *Examples*: quickly, lately, soon, quietly, slowly.

4 **Apostrophes** have two uses.
  a They show **ownership**. When something belongs to someone (or something), the ownership is shown with 's. *Examples*: Rob's game, the dog's collar; the car's tyre; our dentist's fee; the shop's window.
  b They are used for **contractions** (shortened words). When letters are left out of a word, an apostrophe is put their place. *Examples*: was not → wasn't, he will → he'll, they are → they're, I am → I'm, it is → it's, will not → won't (note the change in spelling here)

Note: The word <u>it's</u> stands for 'it is' (e.g. <u>It's</u> a fine day.) Without an apostrophe, <u>its</u> works as a pronoun, just like 'her' and 'his'. (e.g. The cat licked <u>its</u> fur.)

Test Your Skills

1 Underline four more **pronouns** in this passage. (Pronouns 'stand in' for nouns.)
Brad and Kel stopped by the tree. <u>They</u> looked up at the branches. It was a really tall tree. Kel thought he could see a bird's nest. He pointed it out to Brad.

2 Underline five more **prepositions** in this passage. (Prepositions show where things happen.)
Buster climbed <u>onto</u> a box and peered into the shed. There were ropes hanging on the wall, bags stacked in the corner and an oil drum by the door. Then he saw his bike under the bench.

3 Underline three more **adverbs** in this passage. (Adverbs tell how things happen.)
Kent jumped <u>quickly</u> onto the deck. He landed heavily and twisted his ankle. He didn't have much time. Suddenly he heard a cabin door slam. Soon the boat would be leaving.

4 Choose the correct **preposition** to fill the spaces.
  a The crocodile swam _____ the centre of the river to the bank. (in, to, from)
  b When Larry finished eating, he pushed his chair _____ the table. (in, by, under)

5 Write these words in their shortened form.
I am _____   it is _____   we are _____   cannot _____

6 Write these shortened words the long way
you're _____   he's _____   hasn't _____   they're _____

7 Write things that might be owned by these people or animals.
Mum's _____   parrot's _____   butcher's _____   horse's _____

Real Test

GRAMMAR AND PUNCTUATION
Adverbs, prepositions, pronouns and apostrophes

15 min

1 Which of the following correctly completes this sentence?

Tonight Natalie _____ going to get the prize for swimming!

is	are	were	was
A	B	C	D

2 Which of the following correctly completes this sentence?

The train was slow and it took _____ hour to get to Richmond.

a	the	an	in
A	B	C	D

3 Which of the following correctly completes this sentence?

When _____ my turn, get ready to cheer.

tis	its	it's	its'
A	B	C	D

4 Which of the following correctly completes this sentence?

The truck was going _____ around the corner and it slid on the gravel.

quick	quicker	quickally	quickly
A	B	C	D

5 Which of the following correctly completes this sentence?

A branch _____ off the tree and just missed the dog.

break	broke	breaked	breaking
A	B	C	D

6 Which of the following correctly completes this sentence?

Driving _____ the bend we suddenly saw the sea.

around	on	through	in
A	B	C	D

7 How many commas should be used in this sentence?
On our holiday we saw lighthouses museums markets bridges and towers.

none	one	two	three
A	B	C	D

Read the text *Our Newspaper*. The text has some gaps. Choose the best option to fill each gap.

Our Newspaper

We get a newspaper every day.

Today, _____ the paper, I saw a story

8
in	on	at	above
A	B	C	D

about a woman _____ had seen a strange

9
what	which	who	that
A	B	C	D

craft land on her lawn. A door opened _____

10
slow	slowly	slowally	slower
A	B	C	D

and _____ alien emerged in a green light.

11
a	the	an	that
A	B	C	D

☞ **Answers and explanations on page 151**

GRAMMAR AND PUNCTUATION
Adverbs, prepositions, pronouns and apostrophes

_____ face was blank. It had no eyes,

⑫　　　its　　It's　　it's　　Its
　　　　　A　　　B　　　C　　　D

ears, nose _____ even a mouth.

⑬　　　or,　　or　　and,　　, and
　　　　　A　　　B　　　C　　　D

⑭ Which of the following correctly completes the sentence?

There was _____ in the church but we couldn't see who it was.

　　Somebody　　some body　　some-body　　somebody
　　　　A　　　　　　B　　　　　　C　　　　　　D

⑮ Which sentence has the correct punctuation?
　A I can't go and you won't be going?
　B I can't go and you wont be going.
　C I can't go and you won't be going!
　D I ca'nt go and you wo'nt be going!

⑯ Which of the following correctly completes the sentence?

My sight is much _____ since I started wearing glasses.

　　good　　　gooder　　best　　better
　　　A　　　　　B　　　　　C　　　　D

⑰ Shade a bubble to show where the missing comma (,) should go.
For days ▲ weeks ▲ and months ▲ we put up with drought ▲ and dust.
　　　　Ⓐ　　　Ⓑ　　　　Ⓒ　　　　　　　　　　　Ⓓ

⑱ Which sentence is correct?
　A Did you squash me banana?
　B Did you squash my banana?
　C Did you squash my banana!
　D Did you squash mine banana?

☞ **Answers and explanations on page 151**

Test Your Skills

READING
Following procedures

8 min

A procedure is a set of instructions on how to do something. The instructions are often called 'steps'. Procedures will often include materials and tools needed and helpful hints. A recipe is a common form of procedure.

Read the instructions on how to make Chocolate Milk Drift and answer the questions.
Circle the correct answer.

Ingredients

3 teaspoons <u>instant</u> chocolate powder

$\frac{1}{2}$ cup hot water

4 cups cold milk
2 tablespoons chocolate milkshake flavouring
4 scoops chocolate ice-cream

Note: Sugar may be added for individual taste.

Steps
1. Using a coffee mug, dissolve the chocolate powder in hot water. Stir with a spoon if necessary.
2. Pour into a bowl and add the milk. Stir gently.
3. Stir in chocolate flavouring (and sugar if required).
4. Put bowl into fridge and chill.
5. Remove from fridge and whip until foamy.
6. Take out four tall glasses, and put one scoop of ice-cream into each glass.
7. Fill each glass with the chilled chocolate mixture.
8. Drop in a fancy straw and it's ready to enjoy!

For fun, you can float a Smartie, cherry or small strawberry on the foamy surface and let it drift around.

---

1 How many steps are needed to make the Chocolate Milk Drift ready for serving?
  A four   **B** five   **C** eight   **D** twelve

2 Which ingredient might be left out by some people?
  A sugar   **B** ice-cream   **C** flavouring   **D** hot water

3 In the recipe, the word 'instant' means
  A quickly.   **B** ready for use.   **C** this moment.   **D** prepared.

4 Which word could be best replace the word 'Steps'?
  A stairs   **B** levels   **C** stages   **D** method

5 What should be done after chocolate flavouring (and sugar) has been stirred in? The mixture is
  A poured into a glass.   **B** chilled in a fridge.
  C added to scoops of ice-cream.   **D** topped with Smarties, cherries or strawberries.

6 How many serves of Chocolate Milk Drift does this recipe make?
  A three   **B** four   **C** five   **D** six

7 Which of the following materials is **NOT** required to prepare the drink?
  A saucepan   **B** bowl   **C** coffee mug   **D** glass

Answers: 1C 2A 3B 4D 5B 6B 7A

☞ **Explanations on pages 151-152**

Real Test

If you like trying your own magic tricks, here's something for you! Read these instructions on how to impress your friends with The Disappearing Assistant and answer the questions. Circle the correct answer.

You will need ...
- a space or stage some distance from your audience
- a large cardboard box <u>adapted</u> for your show
- an assistant.

How to begin
Tell your audience that you have a brave assistant who you can make disappear. Introduce your assistant to the audience.

Method
1. Tell your assistant to step into the box.
2. Close the lid.
3. Wave your arms over the box and say some magic words, such as 'Going, going, gone!'
4. Tip your box forward towards the audience and lift the cover. The box will be empty.

How it's done—the secret revealed!
First, the box has to be made suitable for your magic.
1. Cut around the bottom on three sides and push the bottom into the box.
2. Fold the bottom flap up into the box.
3. Attach a handle to the bottom using tape.
4. When the assistant steps in she is standing on the floor.
5. When you tip the box towards the audience, the assistant pulls the bottom back into place and crouches behind the box.

1 This information is for people
   A playing a trick.   B learning magic.   C in a TV show.   D in a craft lesson.

2 The word 'assistant' could best be replaced with the word
   A actor.   B helper.   C worker.   D student.

3 Why is the bottom of the box made into a flap?
   A to let the assistant escape   B to provide a place for a handle
   C to give the assistant a place to hide   D to make a top when it is tipped forward

4 Why is it best to perform this act 'some distance from your audience'?
   A to let the assistant escape.   B to make more room for the audience.
   C to keep the assistant out of sight.   D to conceal mistakes made by the magician.

5 Which statement is true?
   A The assistant knows what will happen to him or her.
   B The act is unplanned and not rehearsed.
   C The magic words make the assistant disappear.
   D The audience most likely know how the trick works.

6 When it is stated that the box has been 'adapted', it means that the box
   A can only be used once.   B is given to someone who wants it.
   C has been destroyed.   D has been changed slightly.

☞ **Answers and explanations on page 152**

Book blurbs often appear on the backs of books. They are meant to encourage a person to read the book or buy the book.

Study the blurb from the back of a book called *Bubble Buster* and answer the questions. Circle the correct answer.

1 *Bubble Buster* is one book in a set of

  A four books.
  B seven books.
  C eight books.
  D nine books.

2 The books in this set are most likely meant to

  A amuse the reader.
  B inform the reader.
  C describe true events.
  D explain how to read and write.

3 Books can be set in many places. Which of these books is most likely set on a farm?

  A *Dog Food*
  B *A Hairy Question*
  C *Mandy Made Me Do It*
  D *Look Out! Look Out! Tractor About!*

4 If a reader was interested in sport, which book would he or she be most likely to choose?

  A *Bubble Buster*
  B *Zac's Story*
  C *Mandy Made Me Do It*
  D *Ali's Top Secret Diary*

When Buster starts making bubbles, they get bigger and bigger. Soon he is trapped in a super bubble way above the city. Will Buster get home again?

ISBN 1-86509-321-1

Easy to Read
Hard to Put Down

5 The books are described as 'Hard to Put Down'. What is meant by this?

  A The books are heavy.
  B The books are fun to read.
  C The books are full of pictures.
  D The books are not very well made.

6 At the top of the cover is some information about the story of *Bubble Buster*. It ends with the question 'Will Buster get home?' The question

  A is meant to frighten the reader.
  B means that no one has read the book.
  C means that the story hasn't got a good ending.
  D aims to make the reader want to find out what happens.

7 The books in this set are called Sparklers. What are real sparklers?

  A fireworks
  B stars
  C bubbles
  D fairy lights

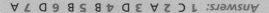

Answers: 1 C 2 A 3 D 4 B 5 B 6 D 7 A

☞ **Explanations on page 152**

Real Test

READING
Interpreting other texts

Read the story *The Wind and the Sun* and answer the questions. Circle the correct answer.

Long, long ago, at the start of the world, the wind and the sun were talking about things they saw when a <u>dispute</u> arose between them. Each felt he was stronger than the other.

How could they find out who was right? After much thought they decided that a contest would be the best and easiest way to find out who was stronger.

Then they wondered what sort of contest they could have. They had no ideas until they saw an old traveller passing by. They agreed to see which one could take his coat off first. The wind was sure he would win.

They agreed that the wind would go first. He began to blow with all his might. He delivered a cold and fierce blast of air that chilled the man right through. The man clutched his coat tightly around his body. Then the wind tried to blow the coat off the man's back, but the stronger the wind became, the more determined the traveller was, and hugged his coat close. He pulled it tightly around his body and his neck, keeping much of the wind out.

Exhausted, the wind let the sun have a go. Breaking out from behind a cloud, the sun let his warm beams spread over the traveller.

The traveller began to feel warmer. The chill left his bones. He sighed, sat down on a rock beside the edge of the road and let his coat drop to the ground.

The wind then knew the sun had won the contest.

1 Which word best describes how the wind felt before the contest?

    A worried   **B** foolish   **C** confident   **D** doubtful

2 What type of story is *The Wind and the Sun*?

    A a fairy tale   **B** a report   **C** a legend   **D** a fable

3 What can a reader learn from this story?

    A All is fair in love and war.   **B** Truth is stranger than fiction.
    C Persuasion is better than force.   **D** Many hands make light work.

4 Choose the best word to fill the space in the following sentence.
The traveller (_____?_____) the wind's efforts to remove his coat.

    A avoided   **B** withstood   **C** ignored   **D** helped

5 How did the traveller get involved in the dispute? Write your answer on the lines.

_____

_____

6 Which word has a similar meaning to the word 'dispute' in the story?

    A disagreement   **B** displease   **C** compete   **D** row

7 Which word would best describe the wind and sun?

    A competitors   **B** enemies   **C** criminals   **D** fighters

☞ **Answers and explanations on page 153**

Study this extract from a report called *Celebrations* by Ida Chionh and answer the questions.

Dragon Boat Festival

The Dragon Boat festival traditionally happens on the fifth day of the fifth month in the Chinese lunar calendar (around June).

The story behind this Chinese festival goes back hundreds of years. There was a poet named Qu Yuan, who was angry with the behaviour of China's government at that time. In protest, Qu Yuan threw himself into the Mi Lo River.

The local fishermen were so moved by his action that they raced in their boats to recover his body. They beat the water with their paddles to scare the fish away from the body. People threw rice dumplings wrapped in silk into the river, to help the poet's spirit to go to heaven.

It soon became a tradition to remember the event with boat races. Boats were often designed to look like dragons, to please the spirit of the waters.

Nowadays dragon boat races are held in many countries, including Australia. They are noisy and colourful occasions. Teams compete for a place in the international races, which are held in Hong Kong and Singapore in June.

1 Why did Qu Yuan throw himself into the river?
  A   He was annoyed with the fishermen.
  B   He wanted to be in a boat race.
  C   He had been frightened by spirits.
  D   He was protesting about the government's behaviour.

2 Why was the food thrown into the water? The food was meant to
  A   feed the fish.
  B   help Qu Yuan swim back to shore.
  C   help the poet's spirit go to heaven.
  D   for the fishermen rescuing Qu Yuan.

3 What happened to Qu Yuan?
  A   He drowned.   B   He was eaten by fish.
  C   He began the dragon boat races.   D   He was rescued by fishermen.

4 How often are dragon boat races held?
  A   monthly   B   five times a year   C   yearly   D   every five years

5 The Chinese racing boats were built to look like
  A   spirits.   B   dragons.   C   fish.   D   fishing boats.

6 Which word has a similar meaning to traditionally?
  A   usually   B   noisily   C   always   D   yearly

☞ **Answers and explanations on page 153**

TIPS FOR WRITING DESCRIPTIONS

Descriptions function as pictures in words of people, places or things. In a description you aim to give the reader a clear and vivid picture of what you are describing. After reading your description the reader should be able to close his or her eyes and picture the subject.

Descriptions are seldom written to stand alone in the same way as, say, narratives or recounts. Descriptions are often part of another kind of writing; they help to make other text types interesting.

When writing descriptions, it is best to keep the following points in mind. They will help you get the best possible mark.

Before you start writing

- Read the question and check the stimulus material carefully. *Stimulus material* means the topic, title, picture, words, phrases or extract of writing you are given to base your writing on.
- Decide how you are going to present your description. It could be in the first person or third person. Take care when using the first person not to overuse the pronoun *I*.
- Decide on the tense you are going to use. Descriptions are usually written in the present tense but feel free to use past or future tenses if this suits your purpose.

The introduction

- Introduce the subject early in your writing. The title should put the subject in focus.

The body

- **Always include some facts.** Descriptions in an information report may consist entirely of facts.
- **Don't just focus on what can be seen.** Enhance your writing by adding 'imagined' sounds and smells—you can even describe how something feels.
- **Make full use of adjectives and adverbs.** Use a short series of adjectives to paint a vivid picture.
- **Use action verbs to describe behaviour.** This adds interest to your description.
- **Use figurative language such as similes and metaphors** to make your description clear and interesting. Avoid clichés.

The conclusion

The final paragraph may include some brief personal opinions in your description—the best place for this is often in the form of a concluding comment.

When you have finished writing give yourself a few minutes to read through your description. Quickly check spelling and punctuation, and insert any words that have been accidentally left out.

WRITING
Description of a place or scene

There is no way of knowing for certain what type of writing will be included in NAPLAN tests in years to come. This is an opportunity for you to practise different types of writing.

Before you start, read the General writing tips on pages 20–21 and the Tips for writing descriptions on page 87.

The aim of a description is to give the reader a clear and vivid word picture of a person, thing, place or scene. Descriptions of scenes are often important in narratives. They can help create different moods and atmosphere.

Today you are going to write a description of A BEACH. Think about the beach, the sea and what surrounds the beach. Start your description with a sentence naming what you are about to describe. Then think about colours and sounds. Think about how the beach is used. Is it an isolated beach or is it a very popular beach? Is it an ocean beach or a river beach? Does it have a surf club or is it used by people fishing? What is on the sand? What birds are sharing the beach with people? Is the weather important?

Before you start writing, give some thought to:
- what you are describing
- the special features of the beach
- how you feel about the way the beach is used.

Don't forget to:
- plan your description before you start writing.
- write in correctly formed sentences and take care with paragraphing
- choose your words carefully and pay attention to your spelling and punctuation
- write neatly but don't waste time
- quickly check your description once you have finished.

Start writing here.

_____

_____

_____

_____

_____

_____

_____

_____

_____

_____

☞ **Marking guide on page 154**

Real Test and Tips

WRITING
Description of a person

There is no way of knowing for certain what type of writing will be included in NAPLAN tests in years to come. This is an opportunity for you to practise different types of writing.

Before you start, read the General writing tips on pages 20–21 and the Tips for writing descriptions on page 87.

The aim of a description is to give the reader a clear and vivid word picture of a person, thing, place or scene. Descriptions of scenes are often important in narratives. They can help create different moods and atmosphere.

Today you are going to write a description of A GRANDPARENT (or an older friend). Think about what makes your grandparent interesting or different. You can write about the person's appearance. Think about their hair, eyes, their stature (height and size) and anything you notice or remember about them. Then think about their mannerisms (the way they do things), habits and their behaviour. Think about what they like doing and what seems to upset them. What do they like to wear? What do they do for relaxation? How do they speak? Are they noisy or quiet? Do they have a hobby?

Before you start writing, give some thought to:
- who you are describing
- where the grandparent spends time
- how you or other family members relate to the grandparent.

Don't forget to:
- plan your description before you start writing.
- write in correctly formed sentences and take care with paragraphing
- choose your words carefully and pay attention to your spelling and punctuation
- write neatly but don't waste time
- quickly check your description once you have finished.

Start writing here.

_____

_____

_____

_____

_____

_____

_____

_____

_____

☞ **Marking guide on pages 154-155**

Real Test and Tips

WRITING
Explanation

There is no way of knowing for certain what type of writing will be included in NAPLAN tests in years to come. This is an opportunity for you to practise different types of writing.

Before you start, read the General writing tips on pages 20–21.

Explanation texts tell how something works or how it is used. Explanations have several parts. These include: a title, a sentence (or two) about what is to be explained, and information on the object or event. An explanation can conclude with a personal comment. Today you are going to write an explanation for A VASE. Think about a vase you have seen regularly. It may be at home, in the school or in an office. Describe it briefly in its setting then tell how it is used. Why is it used where it is? Who looks after it? Is it used as it should be used? It may be important to know where it came from or who owns it. What is attractive about the vase when it is in use? Think about colours and smells.

Before you start writing, give some thought to:
- what you are explaining
- the special features of the vase
- the problems or advantages of having the vase.

Don't forget to:
- plan your explanation before you start writing.
- write in correctly formed sentences and take care with paragraphing
- choose your words carefully and pay attention to your spelling and punctuation
- write neatly but don't waste time
- quickly check your explanation once you have finished.

Start writing here.

_____

_____

_____

_____

_____

_____

_____

_____

_____

_____

☞ **Marking guide on page 155**

How will we go?

Sample Test Papers

Today you are going to write a persuasive text, often called an exposition.

The purpose of writing a persuasive text is to influence or change a reader's thoughts or opinions on a particular topic or subject. Your aim is to convince a reader that your opinion is sensible and logical. Successful persuasive writing is always well planned. Persuasive texts may include advertisements, letters to newspapers, speeches and newspaper editorials, as well as arguments in debates.

A box of tissues should be supplied for each Year 3 student's desk.

What do you think about this idea? Do you support or reject this idea? Write to convince a reader of your opinions.

Before you start writing, give some thought to:
- whether you strongly agree or strongly disagree with this plan
- reasons or evidence for your arguments
- a brief but definite conclusion—list some of your main points and add a personal opinion
- the structure of a persuasive text, which begins with a well-organised introduction, followed by a body of arguments or points, and finally a conclusion that restates the writer's position.

Don't forget to:
- plan your writing before you start—make a list of important points you wish to make
- write in correctly formed sentences and take care with paragraphing
- choose your words carefully, and pay attention to your spelling and punctuation
- write neatly but don't waste time
- quickly check your persuasive text once you have finished—your position must be clear to the reader.

Remember: the stance taken in a persuasive text is not wrong, as long as the writer has evidence to support his or her opinion. How the opinion is supported is as important as the opinion itself.

Start writing here.

_____

_____

_____

_____

_____

_____

_____

_____

_____

☞ **Marking guide on pages 155-156 and sample response on page 23**

The spelling mistakes in these sentences have been highlighted.
Write the correct spelling for each highlighted word in the box.

1 Dad replaced the bored that was starting to rot.

2 I had to bandage the cut to keep out jerms.

3 "That's the laest of my worries!" said Mum.

4 Is Deni training to be a pilote?

5 The test result was a schock.

6 Your house is brick and ourse is timber.

7 We were told to cross at the zebera crossing.

8 My mobile phone is hopless in a tunnel!

9 There are four ponys in the field across the road.

10 The photo was of a veiw from the tower.

The spelling mistakes in these labels have been highlighted.
Write the correct spelling for each of these words in the boxes.

11 air force jet plain

12 caben

13 sweept back wing

14

tale fin

Read the text *Teeth*. Each line has a word that is incorrect.
Write the correct spelling in the box.

Teeth

15 Teeth are our tules for eating: slicing,

16 biteing and grinding food. They are shaped

17 differently to do different tarsks. When you eat

18 an applle, you slice a piece then grind it up.

☞ **Answers and explanations on pages 156-160**

Read the text *Grade 3*. Each line has a word that is incorrect.
Write the correct spelling of the word in the box.

Grade 3

19 Ms Black pointed at the tabel and said, "Grade 3

20 put your show entrys on the far end please."

21 Ms Black beleved that all her children should

22 enter somethink in the school's craft show.

Read the text *Amanda's Cake*. Each line has a word that is incorrect.
Write the correct spelling of the word in the box.

Amanda's Cake

23 Amanda lifted the cover off her plait. Underneath

24 was a perfect carot cake. The icing was light

25 orange with darker orange specks all threw it.

26 Choose the word that is not required in this sentence.
We will plan ahead for our next holiday soon.

will	plan	ahead	next
A	B	C	D

27 Which of the following correctly completes this sentence?
Judy is the student [____] raised the alarm

what	which	who	that
A	B	C	D

28 Which group of words can all be used as adjectives?
A fast, merry, lazy, faithful
B truck, tram, taxi, cart
C buy, loose, cheat, were
D fairly, honestly, only, gully

29 Which of the following correctly completes this sentence?
People have [____] and dogs have paws.

foot	feet	foots	feets
A	B	C	D

30 Which of the following correctly completes this sentence?
Jay plodded steadily [____] the finish line just ahead of her rivals.

beside	at	towards	into
A	B	C	D

☞ **Answers and explanations on pages 156-160**

31 Shade a bubble to show where the missing question mark (?) should go.
"It's not ours but do ⌃ you want to use it ⌃ " ⌃ asked ⌃ Brendan.
Ⓐ   ⒷⒸ   Ⓓ

32 Which of the following correctly completes this sentence?

You did do your corrections, ▨▨▨▨ you?

didn't	do	did	have
A	**B**	**C**	**D**

Read the text *The Bullock Driver*. The text has some gaps.
Choose the best option to fill each gap.

The Bullock Driver

My mate, old Charlie, was a bullock driver.

In the early days ▨▨▨ white settlement

33
at	in	on	of
A	**B**	**C**	**D**

in Australia there weren't many trains ▨▨▨

34
and	or	nor	but
A	**B**	**C**	**D**

trucks. Heavy loads ▨▨▨ hauled by

35
were	was	is	are
A	**B**	**C**	**D**

bullock ▨▨▨ Every month Charlie would

36
team	teams	teams.	team's
A	**B**	**C**	**D**

load up with supplies for ▨▨▨ logging

37
them	the	a	that
A	**B**	**C**	**D**

camps. He ▨▨▨ timber back for the mills.

38
bring	bought	brang	brought
A	**B**	**C**	**D**

39 Which sentence has the correct punctuation?
 A Jim's shoes were dropped in the park and now James can't find them.
 B Jims shoes were dropped in the park and now James can't find them.
 C Jim's shoes were dropped in the park and now Jame's can't find them.
 D Jims shoes were dropped in the park and now Jame's can't find them.

40 Which sentence has the correct punctuation?
 A Whatever the Season, weekends in December are my favourite time.
 B Whatever the Season, Weekends in December are my favourite time.
 C Whatever the Season, weekends in december are my favourite time.
 D Whatever the season, weekends in December are my favourite time.

41 Which of the following correctly completes the sentence?

Sue broke her tooth when she ▨▨▨ into the pork chop.

bite	bitten	bit	bited
A	**B**	**C**	**D**

☞ **Answers and explanations on pages 156-160**

42 Which of the following correctly completes the sentence?

Leanne had hurt her wrist ⬚⬚⬚⬚⬚ she was still able to make pancakes.

as	however	so	if
A	**B**	**C**	**D**

43 Shade a bubble to show where the missing full stop (.) should go.

Jill and ⬆A I don't have hiking boots ⬆B We have backpacks ⬆C and all ⬆D our other clothes.

Ⓐ   Ⓑ   Ⓒ   Ⓓ

44 Which sentence has the correct punctuation?
A   The tree which was struck, by lightning, will have to be removed.
B   The tree, which was struck, by lightning will have to be removed.
C   The tree, which was struck by lightning, will have to be removed.
D   The tree, which, was struck by lightning, will have to be removed.

45 Which word is unnecessary in this sentence?
The two twins were in the same class in primary school.

two	same	the	primary
A	**B**	**C**	**D**

46 Which sentence is correct?
A   The day was cold and there were any people on the beach.
B   The day was cold and there were little people on the beach.
C   The day was cold and there were few people on the beach.
D   The day was cold and there were much people on the beach.

47 Shade one bubble to show where the missing speech mark (") should go.

Ⓐ   Ⓑ   Ⓒ   Ⓓ

As Tyron ⬇A climbed up the ladder ⬇B he shouted ⬇C to his mother, ⬇D How much higher?"

48 Which of the following correctly completes this sentence?

After the warm day, and the sun had gone down, it started to ⬚⬚⬚⬚⬚ off.

cold	cool	change	drop
A	**B**	**C**	**D**

49 Which of the following correctly completes this sentence?

Jill is faster than Cara but Cara is ⬚⬚⬚⬚⬚ than anyone in my team.

fastest	fast	faster	more faster
A	**B**	**C**	**D**

50 Which of the following correctly completes this sentence?

I ⬚⬚⬚⬚⬚ every sum in the book!

have done	have did	has done	done
A	**B**	**C**	**D**

☞ **Answers and explanations on pages 156-160**

Read the extract from *Animal Reports* by Peter Sloan & Ross Latham and answer questions 7–12.

Dingo

The dingo is a canine mammal. It is the Australian wild dog.

The dingo is about as big as a medium sized dog. It has an alert face, sharp, erect ears and a bushy tail. The teeth of the dingo are longer and slimmer than those of other canines.

This canine is usually ginger in colour with white points (eg, feet, the snout and tips of the tail). Sometimes the dingo is black with tan points. It is seldom white.

Dingos are found all over the Australian continent but not in Tasmania.

The dingo is a diurnal (day) hunter. It hunts alone or in packs. If small prey are plentiful, the dingo will hunt alone. In order to capture large animals, dingos work in groups.

Sometimes livestock, such as sheep are attacked, but farm animals make up a very small part of the food eaten by dingos.

The female dingo can give birth to between one and eight pups in a litter, three or four times a year.

7 The word canine is the name for types of

  A dingos.   B sheep.   C pups.   D dogs.

8 What colour are most dingos?

  A ginger   B white   C black   D tan

9 The dingo has erect ears. This means its ears

  A bend over.   B are floppy.   C stand up.   D are large.

10 What is the name given for the ends of the dingo's snout, ears and feet?

  A tips   B points   C tail   D edges

11 Dingos are sometimes described as pack animals. This means

  A female dingos have a large number of pups.
  B many dingos live in the same place.
  C they keep close together when attacked.
  D they hunt as a group.

12 Which statement is true of female dingos?

  A Female dingos have litters of different numbers
  B Female dingos give birth to pups eight times each year
  C Female dingos are often white in colour
  D Female dingos have white feet and black snouts

☞ **Answers and explanations on page 160**

Read the extract and answer questions 13–17.

A Pirate's Life

Who became a pirate? People became pirates for different reasons. Many of them were wanted men: men who had committed a crime and fled to escape punishment. Punishments hundreds of years ago were cruel. A desperate man might be hanged for stealing food so that his family would not starve. To escape the law, many men ran away. The quickest way to run away was to join the crew of a ship – often a pirate ship. Sailors became pirates too. Life at sea was hard and work and the hours were long. Sailors had to survive in rat-infested cabins and eat food that was bad. Sailors sometimes jumped ship to join a pirate crew. Life with pirates on the high seas was more relaxed – and they got a share of the plunder! Trading ships were crammed with valuable goods being delivered from distant land to wealthy merchants. Merchants traded in goods that were not readily available in Europe. Merchants' ships might carry gold, silver, coins, perfumes and even carpets. Then there was ivory from Africa, spices from the East Indies, silk from China and cotton from India. Every merchant's ship was a temptation to pirates.

Goods stolen from ships were called booty. The pirate captain rewarded his crew with a share of the booty in return for their hard work and brave fighting. The captain, being in command, kept the largest share for himself.

13 A 'wanted' man is a man wanted by
- A a pirate captain.
- C the police.
- B a prisoner.
- D a merchant seaman.

14 'Plunder' is a name for
- A running away.
- C temptation.
- B stolen goods.
- D life at sea.

15 Which word best describes life for many people hundreds of years ago?
- A harsh
- C safe
- B tempting
- D wicked

16 Pay for a pirate was better than pay for sailor because a
- A sailor often committed a crime.
- B pirate was given better food than a sailor.
- C sailor lived with rats on his ship.
- D pirate got a share of the stolen goods.

17 Booty is a name for
- A goods stolen from ships at sea.
- B leaving a ship without permission.
- C pirates' footware.
- D food on pirates' ships.

☞ **Answers and explantions on pages 160-161**

Read the extract and answer questions 18–22.

Houseboats

Some people live on boats instead of houses.

A houseboat has doors, windows, walls and a roof just like a normal house. Inside there are different rooms, like a kitchen, bathroom, living room and bedrooms. The floor is built on the houseboat's flat-bottom hull.

A houseboat resembles a house in many ways; however, a houseboat can be moved around and moored where it suits the owner.

The Chinese developed a boat called the junk thousands of years ago. It is still used today – often as a houseboat, and also as a cargo boat or passenger boat.

18 A houseboat would NOT be suitable for
- A   sheltered bays.
- B   inland lakes.
- C   ocean voyages.
- D   broad rivers.

19 The word 'moored' means
- A   resting on sand.
- B   tied up.
- C   costly.
- D   moving freely.

20 Houseboat owners would have difficulty
- A   using a mobile phone.
- B   in wet weather.
- C   learning to swim.
- D   growing a garden.

21 A houseboat would be most suitable for
- A   a retired person.
- B   a couple with a baby.
- C   a family with primary school children.
- D   an elderly couple.

22 A junk
- A   can only be used in China.
- B   can be used as a passenger boat.
- C   does not have sleeping accommodation.
- D   does not carry cargo.

☞ **Answers and explanations on page 161**

Read the back and front covers of *Dog on a Diet* by Joan Dalgleish and answer questions 23–28.

23 The book *Dog on a Diet* is most likely
 A   a fairy tale.
 C   an amusing story.
 B   a true adventure.
 D   a legend.

24 What was Joan Dalgleish before she became a children's author? Write your answer on the line.

_____

25 Who owns the dog on the cover?
 A   Strider Simons
 C   Stephen Axelsen
 B   Joan Dalgleish
 D   Simon James

26 The look on the dog's face on the front cover is one of
 A   satisfaction.
 C   relief.
 B   guilt.
 D   courage.

27 The dog is being put on a diet because
 A   he is getting fat.
 C   Joan Dalgleish no longer works as an actor.
 B   Mr James cannot afford to feed him.
 D   he steals food.

28 The question, What has Strider done now? is added to the back cover blurb because
 A   the writer has forgotten what happened.
 B   the book hasn't been finished.
 C   it will encourage people to buy the book to find the answer.
 D   no one has read the book right through.

☞ **Answers and explanations on page 161**

Read the extract from *Do You Speak English?* by Ida Chionh and answer questions 29–34.

Ben

When Ben started primary school it meant big changes for him. New things to get used to – a new teacher, new lessons, new classmates. Ben grew quieter still.

Ben continued to be a quiet boy during his first year at school. He took part in games when he wanted to. Otherwise he sat in the library corner by himself until his mother picked him up.

At school Ben's teachers worried about him. They tried to get him to join in, but when they spoke to Ben he just refused to join in. Sometimes he would even burst into tears. Ben's parents were worried too. There wasn't anything wrong with Ben. He could read and write and do sums correctly. He was just unhappy.

Show and Tell were the worst times for Ben. He would bring his latest toy or photograph, and then refuse to talk about it.

"Do you want to tell us about your toy?" the teacher would say. "Where did you get it?" or "Who is that man in the photo? Is he your uncle?"

Ben would shake his head and smile, and would not say a word.

29 Ben was a quiet boy. Ben became even quieter because he
- A was getting older.
- B couldn't play school games.
- C spent a lot of time in the library.
- D was not ready for changes in his life.

30 At Show and Tell time Ben would
- A cry.
- B go to the library.
- C shake his head.
- D sit in a corner.

31 Which word best describes Ben?
- A timid
- B cheeky
- C helpful
- D feeble

32 Ben's teachers were
- A upset.
- B considerate.
- C annoyed.
- D impatient.

33 What did Ben take to Show and Tell?
- A his uncle's book
- B a game
- C a photograph
- D a library book

34 Readers are told that Ben could
- A give class reports.
- B take photographs.
- C fix toys.
- D do sums.

☞ **Answers and explanations on page 161**

Read the extract and look at the pictures from *The Tooth Book* by Viki Wright and answer questions 35–40.

Teeth

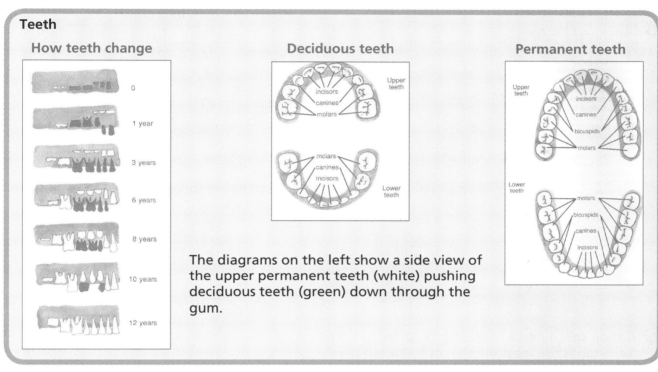

How teeth change

Deciduous teeth

Permanent teeth

The diagrams on the left show a side view of the upper permanent teeth (white) pushing deciduous teeth (green) down through the gum.

35 How many deciduous teeth do babies have inside the upper gum?
  A five
  C sixteen
  B ten
  D twenty

36 By what age do people have most of their permanent teeth? Write your answer on the lines.

_____

_____

37 The largest teeth showing in a one-year-old's mouth are
  A molars.
  C bicuspids.
  B canines.
  D incisors.

38 Which type of teeth do adults have that are not part of the deciduous teeth?
  A molars
  C bicuspids
  B canines
  D incisors

39 The last tooth to come through the upper gum is
  A a molar.
  C a bicuspid.
  B a canine.
  D an incisor.

40 How many deciduous upper teeth are left by age ten?
  A two
  C eight
  B four
  D ten

☞ **Answers and explanations on pages 160-161**

Circle the correct answer.

1 ▭▭▭▭ = 46

What group of squares shows the number 37?

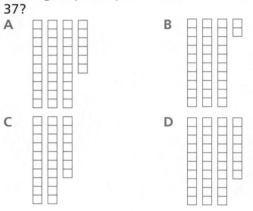

A

B

C

D

2 A shop sells a packet of 8 toilet rolls for $4. What is the most number of toilet rolls Yvonne can buy for $12?

A 3
B 12
C 24
D 32

3

Canteen Price List	
Wrap	$1.85
Sandwich	$1.60
Roll	$2.15
Milk	$1.25
Juice	$1.70

Magenta bought a sandwich and milk from the canteen.
What is the total amount she pays?

$ ▭

4 All four friends are reading the same book. They record the number of pages they read each night over four nights.

	Mon	Tue	Wed	Thur
Amber	16	18	26	30
Bailey	9	13	0	15
Maddie	24	11	6	9
April	23	0	14	18

How many pages did Maddie read on

Wednesday? ▭ pages

5 Which of the following has one half of the shape shaded?

A   B

C   D

6 Theo placed these 10 cent coins in rows of 6.

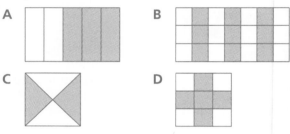

A 1   B 2
C 3   D 4

7 Which building is the tallest?

A   B   C   D

☞ **Answers and explanations on pages 162-164**

8 Conrad walked from the bank to the hospital. Which directions did he follow?

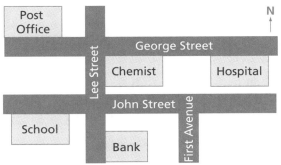

A north along Lee Street and then west along George Street

B north along Lee Street and then east along George Street

C south along Lee Street and then west along George Street

D south along Lee Street and then east along George Street

9 Which of these angles is the largest?

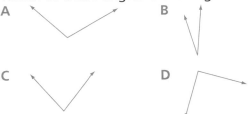

10 Phoebe has $12.55 in her wallet. She needs to save another $3.40 to be able to buy a chain. What is the price of the chain?

$

11 This graph shows the money raised by different year groups at a primary school.

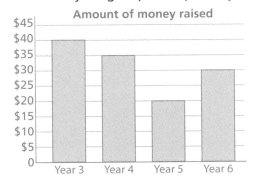

Which statement is true?

A Year 3 raised less money than Year 4

B Year 6 raised more money than Year 3

C Year 5 raised twice as much money as Year 3

D Year 5 raised half as much as Year 3

12 Blake has 28 stickers. He decides to share the stickers between Li and Shane. He gives Li four more stickers than he gives Shane. How many stickers does Shane receive?

A 4

B 12

C 16

D 24

13 A letter X is the same when it is flipped over the dotted line.

Which of these shapes will not look the same when it is flipped over the dotted line?

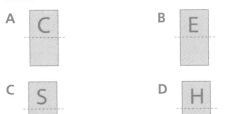

14 Robin drew three shapes. She drew a hexagon and a pentagon and a third shape. She counted a total of 14 sides in the three shapes.

What is the third shape?

A triangle

B pentagon

C hexagon

D octagon

☞ **Answers and explanations on pages 162–164**

15 The table shows the marks scored in a test by four students:

Student	Marks
Maria	78
Kristin	81
Matheus	68
Lucas	74

Which student has a mark closest to 70?
A Maria
B Kristin
C Matheus
D Lucas

16 Miriam grows tomato plants and sells them to her neighbours.
She sells 6 plants for $18.
How many plants will she need to sell to make $12?

Write your answer in the box.

17 Class 3P has 25 students. Ms Petersen, 3P's teacher, drew three circles on the playground.

An equal number of her students moved into each circle. How many students are left over?
A 1
B 2
C 3
D 8

18 This pattern is made by counting forward 19 to each number:

33, 52, 71, ____

Write the next number in the box.

19 Donald wrote these numbers on four cards.

He then added the numbers on **three** of the cards together.

Which of these totals is impossible?
A 7   B 10
C 11   D 12

20 A necklace is to be made up of coloured beads.
Lexie uses red (R) beads, blue (B) beads, yellow (Y) and green (G) beads.

Here is a section of the necklace:

... R B B G Y Y R B B G Y Y R B B G Y Y ...

Lexie repeated this pattern in the necklace. When she had finished, Lexie counted 6 green (G) beads in the completed necklace.
How many yellow (Y) beads did Lexie use in the necklace?
A 3   B 6
C 12   D 24

21 A group of friends compared the number of phone numbers that were stored on their mobile phones.
The results are shown in the table.

Name	Phone numbers
Anthony	42
Logan	27
Valentina	68
Aaron	52
Julieta	63
Alba	48

How many students have more than 50 stored phone numbers?
A 3
B 4
C 6
D 52

☞ **Answers and explanations on pages 162-164**

22 Karl pasted rectangles over the grid. He wants to cover the entire grid with rectangles.

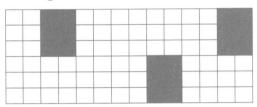

How many more rectangles will Karl need?
A 11
B 12
C 14
D 15

23 At home, Lea has three shelves in her kitchen pantry.
Pasta is on the middle shelf, second from the right.

Top shelf	cereal	sultanas	sugar	coffee	tea
Middle shelf	spreads	soup	spices	pasta	rice
Bottom shelf	foil	bags	wrap	snacks	biscuits

Where is the soup?
A Middle shelf, second from the left
B Bottom shelf, third from the left
C Top shelf, third from the right
D Middle shelf, second from the right

24 John thought of his favourite number.
He doubled the number and subtracted 4.
His answer is 6. What is John's favourite number?

Write your answer in the box.

25 How many triangles are in the shape?

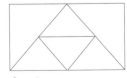

A 4   B 5
C 6   D 7

26 Nicole makes a spinner and puts numbers in each area.

Which statement is not true?
A It is more likely to spin a 3 than a 1
B It is more likely to spin an even number than an odd number
C It is more likely to spin an odd number than an even number
D It is less likely to spin a 1 than a 2

27 After the vacation, the students in Year 3 were asked what movies they had seen during their holidays.
This graph shows four of the more popular movies.

Movies seen by Year 3 students

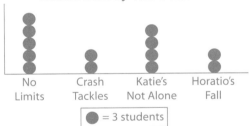

= 3 students

How many students watched *Katie's Not Alone*?
A 3
B 4
C 12
D 13

28 Ashley thought of a number.
She doubled it and subtracted 3.
The answer was 17.
What was the number that Ashley started with?

Write your answer in the box.

☞ **Answers and explanations on pages 162-164**

29 At the school fete, a game of 'Knock 'em Down' is played.
It involves using tennis balls taken from a bucket and thrown at a target.
Each bucket contains 3 tennis balls.

Which of these would find the total number of tennis balls?

A 6 + 3
B 6 − 3
C 6 × 3
D 6 ÷ 3

30 Matti is counting backwards from 157 by twenty. What is the next number?

157   137   117   [   ]

Write the correct answer in the box.

31 Melinda and Brittany support two different teams who play in the same sports competition.
Melinda supports the Blues, and Brittany supports the Reds.
Throughout the season the two teams play each other four times and the results are in the table below.

	Blues	Reds
Game 1	32	20
Game 2	44	38
Game 3	24	36
Game 4	38	22

In how many games did the Blues defeat the Reds by more than 10 points?

A 1   B 2
C 3   D 4

32 What number is half-way between 125 and 165?

125 ————————————————— 165

Write your answer in the box. [   ]

33 A bottle contains 100 vitamin C tablets.
A mother has 3 children.
She gives each of her children 2 tablets every day.
How many tablets remain in the bottle after one week? [   ]

34 Hannah has drawn a shape on a square sheet of paper.

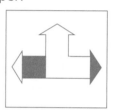

She now turns the paper a quarter turn in the clockwise direction.
What does the page now look like?

A

B

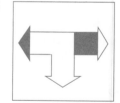

C

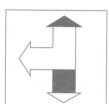

D

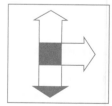

☞ **Answers and explanations on pages 162-164**

35 Andrew used cubes like this  to make a

large cube like this

He then painted the large cube with red paint. After the paint had dried, he pulled the cube apart.

How many of the small cubes have no red faces?

A   1
B   3
C   9
D   12

Read the extract and answer questions 1–6.

Drawing stars

Drawing stars is easy and a great way to decorate books, folders, cards, or anything you want to make distinctly your own. There are two easy stars to start with: the six-pointed and the five-pointed star.

All you need: scraps of paper or unused sections of old school books

a pen, pencil or whatever you prefer to draw with

you might like to have an eraser handy

The six-pointed star

Draw a triangle on your scrap of paper (try to make the sides much the same size)

Now draw a second triangle, the same size, on top of the first triangle. This time draw the triangle upside down.   You can rub out the internal lines if you are happy with your star. Then simply colour your star in.

The five-pointed star

Draw a sloping line.   (The arrowhead is just to show the direction.) Now draw a line going up.   Add the third line.   Now add a fourth line.

Now join the fourth line to the point where you started the first line.

You now have a five-pointed star.   Use your sparkle pens to draw stars for decorations. When you feel confident, try to draw stars starting at any of the five points.

1 How many lines are needed to draw a five-pointed star?
A   four
B   five
C   six
D   ten

2 Before colouring in a star it is best to
A   rub out the inside lines.
C   add the arrow heads to the lines.
B   use a different coloured pen.
D   do all lines with sparkle pens.

3 You will need scrap paper to start with
A   in case the sparkle pens leak.
C   to practise on.
B   so that the table is not marked.
D   to hide any poorly made stars.

4 The lines showing how to draw a five-pointed star have arrowheads on them to show
A   how quickly it is to draw a star.
C   that it is not a six-pointed star.
B   which way each new line goes.
D   people who cannot read what to do.

5 What is suggested you do once you feel confident drawing five-pointed stars?
A   try to draw six-pointed stars
B   draw around the star outline with sparkle pens
C   colour the star to cover the lines
D   try drawing stars starting at different point

6 This passage could best be described as
A   a description.
C   a set of instructions.
B   an explanation.
D   an information report.

☞ **Answers and explanations on page 160**

Before you start, read the general tips on pages 20–21.

The aim of a description is to give the reader a clear and vivid word picture of a person, thing, place or scene. Descriptions of scenes are often important in narratives. They can help create different moods and atmosphere.

Today you are going to write a description of A PARK. Think about a park, what is in it and what surrounds it. Start your description with a sentence naming what you are about to describe. Then think about colours and sounds. Think about how the park is used. Is it a popular park or is it a park that people avoid? Is it a country or city park? Is it a National Park? Does it have rangers? What do people, young and old, do in the park? What animals can be seen in the park? Is the park used in different sorts of weather? How is it used on different days of the week? Is it used for sport, walking dogs, jogging or picnics?

Before you start writing, give some thought to:
- what you are describing
- the special features of the park
- how you feel about the way the park is used.

Don't forget to:
- plan your description before you start writing.
- write in correctly formed sentences and take care with paragraphing
- choose your words carefully and pay attention to your spelling and punctuation
- write neatly but don't waste time
- quickly check your description once you have finished.

Start writing here.

_____

_____

_____

_____

_____

_____

_____

_____

_____

_____

_____

☞ **Marking guide on page 164**

Sample Test Paper

The spelling mistakes in these sentences have been highlighted.
Write the correct spelling for each highlighted word in the box.

1. Max was in the laundery washing his socks.

2. Mum was carefull picking up the broken glass.

3. The wifes were upset by the long working hours.

4. Packed lunchers were prepared that morning.

5. A warning sign was wird to the gate.

6. The visitors looked over the legde.

7. Did the burglar come through the open winder?

8. The game starts in the center of the field.

9. Rex was too hastey to be a good chess player.

10. A long envelop was pushed under our door.

The spelling mistakes in these labels have been highlighted.
Write the correct spelling for each highlighted word in the box.

11. arlarm clock

12. clock fase

13. grene case

14. minet hand

Read the text *Cyclone Tracy*.
Each line has a word that is incorrect. Write the correct spelling in the box.

Cyclone Tracy

15. On Christmas Eve 1974, the poeple of Darwin

16. were worned to get ready for a cyclone.

17. Almost everybody thought the cyclone wood

18. pass end blow out to sea. But at 3 o'clock on

19. Christmas morning the cyclone struk.

20. Strong winds latshed the sleeping city.

☞ **Answers and explanations on pages 164–168**

SAMPLE TEST 2
Literacy—Language conventions

Read the text *Looking After Our Body*.
Each line has a word that is incorrect. Write the correct spelling in the box.

Looking After Our Body

21 We should look after the outside off our body.

22 If it is sunny we can put on a hat and yuse

23 block-out in summer to avoid getting burnt. If we

24 go to the beach it is not wise to lye in the sun.

25 A tan looks good but to much sun is dangerous.

26 Which of the following correctly completes this sentence?

Zara knew the money was not ⬚ !

hers	her	her's	she's
A	**B**	**C**	**D**

27 Which of the following correctly completes this sentence?

Our dog ⬚ up plants in the new garden.

digged	dig	dugged	dug
A	**B**	**C**	**D**

28 Which of the following correctly completes this sentence?

We ⬚ our first party invitation.

has written	have written	have wrote	have writ
A	**B**	**C**	**D**

29 Which of the following correctly completes this sentence?

Come in for lunch now. You can finish the cleaning ⬚ .

soon	yet	later	now
A	**B**	**C**	**D**

30 Which of the following correctly completes this sentence?

The river ⬚ runs through the valley is dry.

how	what	which	who
A	**B**	**C**	**D**

31 Shade two bubbles to show where the missing full stops (.) should go.

On Tuesday, Len is four ⬆ I am not four until next week ⬆ but ⬆ Sara is already five ⬆

Ⓐ　　　　　　　　　Ⓑ　Ⓒ　　　　　　　Ⓓ

☞ **Answers and explanations on pages 164-168**

32 Which of the following correctly completes this sentence?

Mel made his way carefully ▭ the rail from the gate to the shed.

up	into	on	along
A	B	C	D

Read the text *Sir Wally*. The text has some gaps.
Choose the best option to fill each gap.

Sir Wally

Sir Wally was a knight.

He was a fine warrior and often ▭ his

33
led	lead	leaded	let
A	B	C	D

men ▭ fierce battles. He was a friend of

34
onto	into	on	at
A	B	C	D

the king and was rewarded with each ▭

35
victory	victory.	Victory	victory?
A	B	C	D

Did he ever get injured ▭ Only once,

36
,	!	?	.
A	B	C	D

when he ▭ from his horse into a pond.

37
fell	falls	fallen	felled
A	B	C	D

The king just laughed ▭ laughed.

38
an	or	but	and
A	B	C	D

39 Which sentence has the correct punctuation?
- A Australia day celebrations are held in January every year.
- B Australia Day celebrations are held in January every Year.
- C Australia Day celebrations are held in January every year.
- D Australia day celebrations are held in January every Year.

40 Which sentence has the correct punctuation?
- A The captain's orders were to pass all flag's to the leader's.
- B The captain's orders were to pass all flags to the leader's.
- C The captain's order's were to pas's all flags to the leader's.
- D The captain's orders were to pass all flags to the leaders.

41 Which of the following correctly completes the sentence?

We left ▭ black umbrella by the front door.

an	a	and	are
A	B	C	D

☞ **Answers and explanations on pages 164–168**

42 Choose the word that is a preposition in this sentence.
The tourists saw a strange bird as they walked along the cliff track.

strange	as	along	cliff
A	**B**	**C**	**D**

43 Shade two bubbles to show where the missing commas (,) should go.
Can we borrow ⌃books ⌃CDs ⌃magazines ⌃and posters from the town library?
(A)   (B) (C)   (D)

44 Which sentence has the correct punctuation?
A The teacher said, "Is two plus two really five?"
B The teacher said, "Is two plus two really five."
C The teacher said, "is two plus two really five?"
D The teacher said? "Is two plus two really five."

45 Which word or words are unnecessary in this sentence?
I'd like to ask a question about the person who entered our classroom.

a question	about	the person	our
A	**B**	**C**	**D**

46 Which sentence is correct?
A The cat and the dog is good friends.
B The cat and the dog am good friends.
C The cat and the dog are good friends.
D The cat and the dog was good friends.

47 Which sentence has the correct punctuation?
A Jack has his painting. Whose is this one?
B Jack has he's painting. Whose is this one?
C Jack has his painting. Who's this one?
D Jack has his painting? Whose is this one?

48 Which of the following correctly completes this sentence?

Jake is the ▢▢▢ player in his street.

better	best	good	gooder
A	**B**	**C**	**D**

49 Which of the following correctly completes this sentence?

"We don't need this hose ▢▢▢ , " said the gardener, wiping his hands.

anymore	any more	any-more	Anymore
A	**B**	**C**	**D**

50 Which of the following correctly completes this sentence?

I listened to Sam's talk and I ▢▢▢ silent the whole time.

is	are	was	am
A	**B**	**C**	**D**

☞ **Answers and explanations on pages 164-168**

Read the extract and answer questions 1–6.

Snowflakes

It had been snowing all day and I had been bored all day, and getting on Dad's nerves. With a sigh Dad offered to reward me with fifteen dollars if I could find two identical snowflakes. My mood suddenly changed.

When I had captured about twenty snowflakes on a piece of black cardboard I began examining them through the magnifying glass. I was soon to be fifteen dollars richer!

The first two were similar. Both had the six arms like you see in pictures. The next few were totally different. No matches. Still I shouldn't expect instant success.

I was inspecting my second lot when Jasper suddenly arrived from next door.

"Studying snowflake shapes!" he beamed. "Some amazing patterns in snowflakes."

I looked at him from under my eyebrows. He was keeping me from my reward.

"Did you know Krystal," he said, "that no two snowflakes are identical?"

I stopped inspecting, but didn't say anything. Jasper rarely gets his facts wrong.

Slowly I raised my head and nodded, then I glared at our house. Dad was inside warm and cosy fiddling with his model trains. If looks could kill…

I'd been conned but I wasn't going to let Dad know.

"Want to build a snowman?" I suddenly exclaimed.

Jasper put his head to one side. He wasn't expecting that question. "Right. Okay," he agreed suspiciously.

"Why not?" I fired at him. I was still mad at Dad.

"Mine always fall over!"

"We'll make it lying down, Can't fall over then!" I said slickly. For a smart kid, Jasper never thinks of the obvious. Jasper gave a doubtful nod.

1 Who is catching snowflakes?
A Jasper   B Krystal   C Krystal's father   D the snowman

2 When Krystal's dad make his offer of a reward he was being
A tricky.   B cruel.   C serious.   D scientific.

3 Another good title for the passage would be
A Twenty Snowflakes.   B The Snowman.
C Doubtful Jasper.   D Krystal Gets Conned.

4 Which of these shapes is most like a snowflake?
A   B   C   D

5 How did Krystal feel when Jasper told her about snowflake shapes?
A amazed   B confused   C disappointed   D angry

6 Jasper admitted he
A would like to kill Krystal's father.   B could not make a snowman stand up.
C had never found two similar snowflakes.   D preferred to make his snowmen lying down.

☞ **Answers and explanations on page 168**

Read the extract and answer questions 7–12.

Blue Tongue Lizard

Blue Tongue lizards are reptiles. They are found all over Australia. They usually live in open country with lots of ground cover, such as clumps of grass or leaf litter. At night, they shelter among leaf litter, in burrows and under rocks and logs. Early in the morning, Blue Tongues emerge to bask in sunny areas before hunting for food while the day is warm. Blue Tongues do not produce their own body heat. They rely on the sun to keep them warm or they find a warm sheltered spot. In cold weather they are inactive, buried deep in their shelter sites.

The Blue Tongue has a long body, large head and short legs and toes. It is a silvery colour with dark brown bands across the back of the tail and a black stripe between the eyes The belly of the Blue Tongue is a paler colour. Their eyes are small and reddish-brown to grey. The pointed tail is shorter than the body. The Blue Tongue has small overlapping scales on its back. Its blue tongue grows up to 60 cm long. The tongue is dark blue and the lining of the mouth is bright pink.

Blue Tongues eat a wide variety of vegetation and invertebrates (animals without backbones). Their teeth are large and they have strong jaw muscles. They can crush snail shells and beetles. When threatened, a Blue Tongue faces its threat directly, opens its pink mouth wide and sticks out its broad, blue tongue. Because it has a large head for a small creature this may scare off some predators. If the threat does not go away, it hisses and flattens out its body to make itself look bigger.

7 What colour is the mouth of a Blue Tongue lizard?
A   pink
C   black
B   blue
D   reddish brown

8 Blue Tongues like to bask in the sun. This means they
A   sleep when it is sunny.
C   lie in the sun.
B   fight when they get hot.
D   change colour in sunlight.

9 Blue Tongues do NOT eat
A   snails.
C   insects.
B   grass.
D   birds' eggs.

10 Where is the palest part of the Blue Tongue's skin? Write your answer on the lines.

_____

_____

11 The Blue Tongue has
A   a short body.
C   strong jaw muscles.
B   long legs.
D   large eyes.

12 The Blue Tongue scares predators by
A   sticking out its tongue.
C   showing its teeth.
B   making loud noises.
D   clawing at the air.

☞ **Answers and explanations on page 168**

Read the extract and answer questions 13–18.

Knock-down Clown   Time required: 30 minutes
What you need
- Half a tennis ball or similar ball (ask an adult to cut the ball in half using a craft knife before you start)
- Paper • Sticky tape • Round-nose scissors • Coloured pencils or textas

What to do
1 Place the halved tennis ball on a flat surface with the hollow facing up. Push down one side of the ball. You will see that it rolls back to its first position.
2 Add a paper tube to the top of the ball. This will be the clown's body. With sticky tape, attach the paper around the top edge of the ball. The curved part of the half-ball sticks out of the tube. If the tube is too long or is too heavy you will have to make the tube smaller.
3 To adjust: Cut small rings off the paper tube and test whether the clown shape returns to an upright position. Keep cutting small rings off the top until it does.
4 Use coloured pencils to draw a clown on the tube.

What is happening
When the ball is pushed from one side, the ball rolls back to the middle position so the heaviest part of the 'clown' is at lowest point. Attaching a long paper tube adds weight to the upper part of the toy. If the clown does not stand back up after being knocked over, the top is too high so the paper tube needs to be shorter. Cutting rings off the tube reduces its weight.

Science and the clown
Scientists would say that the centre of gravity has been lowered. An object is less likely to fall over if it has a low centre of gravity. Children's blow-up punching toys use this science idea.

13 These instructions could be part of
   A   a set of sports tips.
   C   a book of birthday presents.
   B   an exercise program.
   D   a science experiment.

14 What would be the reason for asking an adult to cut the ball in half?
   A   it requires strong hands
   C   the ball belongs to an adult
   B   craft knives can be dangerous
   D   it requires a very special skill

15 What are the scissors used for?
   A   to trim the paper tube
   C   to cut the sticky tape
   B   to start the cut in the tennis ball
   D   to make a second tube

16 Because the finished clown has a low centre of gravity it
   A   is easy to make.
   C   returns to an upright position if pushed.
   B   will tumble off a workbench top.
   D   will fall over if not made secure.

17 The coloured pencils are used to
   A   cover up mistakes.
   C   draw guide lines.
   B   decorate the tube.
   D   colour the tennis ball.

18 If the paper tube is too long it is best to
   A   make a new tube.
   C   add more sticky tape.
   B   get another type of ball.
   D   trim the paper tube.

☞ **Answers and explanations on page 169**

Read the extract and answer questions 19–25.

Kangaroo Paw

The red and green Kangaroo Paw is Western Australia's state floral emblem. It is the most widespread of all the Kangaroo Paws, occurring in low woodland, forests and on poor sandy soils, gravel, and sometimes in low lying areas such as the fringe of swamps. Kangaroo Paws are only found growing naturally in Western Australia. There are about a dozen different types.

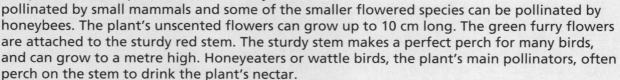

All species are bird pollinated. Some may also be pollinated by small mammals and some of the smaller flowered species can be pollinated by honeybees. The plant's unscented flowers can grow up to 10 cm long. The green furry flowers are attached to the sturdy red stem. The sturdy stem makes a perfect perch for many birds, and can grow to a metre high. Honeyeaters or wattle birds, the plant's main pollinators, often perch on the stem to drink the plant's nectar.

The little hairs on the flower give the flower a bad taste. Predators won't eat the flowers. The little hairs also help by holding on to water because it grows in a dry climate.

Flower colour comes from the coloured hairs which cover the flower, usually on the top part of the flowering stem. The flowering season is from August to November. The long flat leaves are green to greyish green, and about 20 cm long.

19 The hairs on the Kangaroo Paw flower
   A   trap water.
   C   keep bees away.
   B   protect the plant from sunlight.
   D   snare insects.

20 A floral emblem is a
   A   a bunch of Kangaroo Paws.
   C   a badge design based on a flower.
   B   group of flowers grown in a planned garden.
   D   something that resembles a plant.

21 All types of Kangaroo Paws can be pollinated by
   A   birds.
   C   small mammals.
   B   honeybees.
   D   small lizards.

22 The Kangaroo Paw flower is unusual in that it
   A   can only be grown in Western Australia.
   C   flowers between August and November.
   B   has no smell.
   D   grows in a dry climate.

23 The end of the Kangaroo Paw flower looks like a
   A   jug.   B   tub.   C   spider.   D   star.

24 The stem of the Kangaroo Paw flower is
   A   green.   B   black.   C   red.   D   yellow.

25 Kangaroo Paws grow well
   A   in deserts.   B   in sandy soils.
   C   on beaches.   D   on mountain slopes.

☞ **Answers and explanations on page 169**

Look carefully at this circus poster from the 1960s and answer questions 26–31.

26 On which day in January is the circus matinee?
A 21st   B 22nd   C 23rd   D 26th

27 What are the ladies doing on the horses?
A balancing   B sitting   C skipping   D handstands

28 How much is it for a family of five to go to the circus matinee?
A $20   B $22   C $40   D $44

29 What does the stilt walker do?
A lion taming   B juggling   C lift weights   D a trapeze act

30 The clown also
A trains dogs.   B rides horses.   C has a balancing act.   D announces acts.

31 This poster is meant to
A attract people's attention to buy the poster.   B encourage people to join the circus.
C trick people into spending money.   D convince people to go to the circus.

☞ **Answers and explanations on page 169**

Read the extract and answer questions 32–37.

The Computer Swallowed Grandpa

This is a tribute to all the grandparents who have been fearless and learned to use the computer.

The computer swallowed grandpa.
Yes, honestly it's true!
He pressed 'control' and 'enter'
And disappeared from view.

It devoured him completely,
The thought just makes me squirm.
He must have caught a virus
Or been eaten by a worm.

I've searched through the Recycle Bin
And files of every kind;
I've even used the Internet,
But nothing did I find.

In desperation, I asked Google
My searches to refine.
The reply from them was negative,
Not a thing was found 'online'.

So, if inside your 'Inbox,'
My Grandpa you should see,
Please 'Copy', 'Scan' and 'Paste' him
And send him back to me!

Author unknown

32 Grandpa disappeared after he
A used the computer's recycle bin.
B went online.
C pressed 'control' and 'enter' on the computer.
D was taken by a virus.

33 Write the numbers 1 to 4 in the boxes to show the correct order in which events happened in the text. The first one (1) has been done for you.

	Google's help was requested to find grandpa.
1	Grandpa pressed 'control' and 'enter'.
	The narrator searched the Recycle Bin.
	Grandpa vanished.

34 In the introduction, the poem is described as a tribute to all grandparents. A tribute is
A a gift.
B praise.
C a story.
D a reward.

35 The poet has a feeling about grandparents using computers. It is a feeling of
A envy.
B nervousness.
C suspicion.
D respect.

36 The poet uses Google because
A he or she has run out of ideas.
B he or she believes in Google's ability.
C he or she blames Google for the loss.
D all poets use Google to find things.

37 The poem could be described as a
A warning against computer errors.
B plan to find lost data.
C plea for help.
D report on how to find grandparents.

☞ **Answers and explanations on pages 169-170**

Look carefully at this cartoon and answer questions 38–40.

CONFUSION

Wasn't that a great parade?

38 The cartoon is called CONFUSION because
  A   Sally cannot think of an answer to the question.
  B   Sally doesn't know why her mother would ask such a question.
  C   Sally's mother didn't go to the parade.
  D   Sally wasn't allowed to go in the parade.

39 What did Sally see at the parade? Write your answer on the lines.

_____

_____

_____

40 The bubble is used to indicate
  A   that Sally is unable to talk.
  B   what Sally is going to say.
  C   what people wore to the parade.
  D   what Sally can remember.

☞ **Answers and explanations on page 170**

1 What is the mass of a mobile phone?
A   2 grams
B   120 grams
C   10 kilograms
D   200 kilograms

2 Shastri flipped this shape across the dotted line.

What did the new shape look like?
A    B

C    D

3 Peter has coins in his wallet.
He needed to buy lunch, which costs $2.80.
Peter used 5 coins to buy lunch.
Which of the following coins did he use to pay exactly $2.80?

A

B

C

D

4 Which object is a pentagon?
A   B

C   D

5 Which of these has one line of symmetry?

A 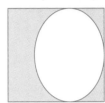   B

C    D

6 Todd added the numbers 45 and 31.
Write Todd's correct answer in the boxes.

4 5 + 3 1 = ☐ ☐

7 Jessie has put some stickers on this grid.
She wants to cover the whole grid with the same stickers.

How many more stickers does she need?
A   6   B   8
C   10   D   12

8 12 × 4 has the same value as
A   24 × 2
B   6 × 6
C   8 × 10
D   6 × 4

9 | 15 | + | 14 | = | 33 | – | ☐ |

Which number should be written in the box to make it correct?
A   4
B   5
C   14
D   15

☞ **Answers and explanations on pages 170-172**

10 Riley's piano lesson started at 5:15 and lasts for 30 minutes.
If the time is now 5:35, how many more minutes are there before the lesson is over?
A 5 minutes
B 10 minutes
C 15 minutes
D 20 minutes

11 A whole number is multiplied by 5.
Which number could not be the answer?
A 85
B 45
C 70
D 53

12 Golf balls are on sale at 3 for $2.
What is the largest number of golf balls that can be bought for $10?
A 5
B 10
C 15
D 30

13 A grid contains letters.
Sasha places a coin on the letter **P**.
She moves the coin 1 square down, 2 squares left and 2 squares up.

top	X	W	V	U	T	S
	M	N	O	P	Q	R
	L	K	J	I	H	G
bottom	A	B	C	D	E	F

Where is Sasha's coin now?
A L
B S
C W
D P

14 Katie drew an octagon inside a hexagon.
Which diagram did she draw?

A    B

C    D

15 The graph shows the number of laps walked by a group of friends in the school's lapathon.

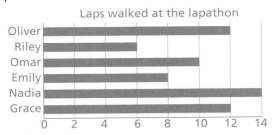

Laps walked at the lapathon

How many laps did Emily and Grace walk in total? Write your answer in the box.

 laps

16 Jocelyn has 16 buttons arranged in 2 rows of eight buttons each.

She changes the arrangement so that she has 4 equal rows.
How many buttons are in each of her rows in the new arrangement?
A 2   B 4
C 6   D 8

17 A grid has been formed using small squares.
Alexi has shaded some of the squares.

How many more squares will Alexi need to shade so that three-quarters of the grid is shaded?
A 3   B 12
C 15   D 21

☞ **Answers and explanations on pages 170–172**

18 The diagram shows a set of scales which are in balance.

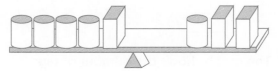

This means that the mass of one 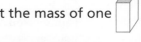 is the same as

A

B

C

D

19 At a concert, ten friends are seated across the first 2 rows in the audience.

2nd row	Daniel	Felix	Dylan	Jade	Sam
1st row	Paula	Hugo	Sara	Fleur	Katalina

Who is sitting in the first row, second from the right?

A Jade   B Fleur
C Hugo   D Katalina

20 Yvette used this number chart to make a pattern of numbers that can be divided by 3.

1	2	3	4	5	6	7	8	9	10
11	12	13	14	15	16	17	18	19	20
21	22	23	24	25	26	27	28	29	30
31	32	33	34	35	36	37	38	39	40
41	42	43	44	45	46	47	48	49	50
51	52	53	54	55	56	57	58	59	60

Yvette continues the pattern of shading. Which of these numbers will be shaded?

A 41   B 46
C 49   D 54

21 This graph shows the way that students came to school today.

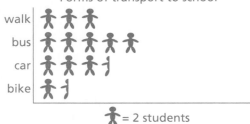

How many students travelled to school in a car?  students

22 Violetta drew a heart and a cross on a square sheet of paper.
She then rotated the paper a quarter turn in the direction of the arrow.

What does the sheet of paper look like?

A   B

C   D

23 Gina cut three and a half apples into quarters.

How many quarters does she have?

A 7
B 11
C 13
D 14

☞ **Answers and explanations on pages 170-172**

24 Diem has these cards.

She uses all the cards to make the largest possible 4-digit number.
Write the number that Diem has made in the box.

25 Sally's mother bought her a pair of jeans for $79 and a pair of shoes for $43.
Which of these gives the best estimate of the total money Sally's mother spent?
A $70 + $40
B $80 + $40
C $80 + $50
D $80 + $30

26 Karen makes six cupcakes and uses four marshmallows to decorate them.
If she makes another batch of 15 cupcakes, how many marshmallows will she need?

Write your answer in the box.

27 The number 1086 can be written as
A Eighteen hundred and six
B One thousand eight hundred and six
C One thousand and eighty six
D Eighteen thousand and six

28 Ralph bought a wallet and a key ring.
He paid a total of $32.
The wallet cost $10 more than the key ring.
What did the key ring cost?

Write your answer in the box. $

29 Suzie has some money to buy lunch.
She buys a salad roll for $2.25.
She still has $1.60 left.
How much money did she start with?

$

30 The next time the arrow is spun, what is the least likely colour it will stop at?

A red
B pink
C green
D yellow

31 Mary has two clocks in her kitchen.
Her wall clock and her microwave clock show different times.

What is the difference in time between the two clocks?

minutes

32 Ellen's chart has stickers in the shape of hearts.

What fraction of the hearts is coloured?

A $\frac{1}{6}$ B $\frac{1}{5}$

C $\frac{2}{5}$ D $\frac{2}{3}$

☞ **Answers and explanations on pages 170–172**

33 A carton holds some boxes.

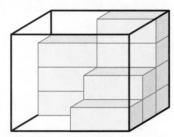

How many **more** boxes can fit into the carton?

Write your answer in the box.

34 Mitchell has many cards with the digits 2, 3 and 4 written on them.

He has equal numbers of cards for each digit.
He lays the cards on a table and adds the digits together to get a total of 36.
How many cards are on the table?

Write your answer in the box.

35 The table shows the number of emails received by 4 girls.

	Mon	Tues	Wed	Thur	Fri
Juliet	3	6	6	4	3
Tara	4	4	8	7	6
Sophie	6	7	5	6	4
Ella	6	7	5	6	4

Who received the most emails in total across the five days?

A Juliet
B Tara
C Sophie
D Ella

☞ **Answers and explanations on pages 170-172**

WEEK 1

1 The 3 is in the hundreds place, so its place value is hundreds.

2 When counting, 39 comes just before 40.

3 64 + 10 = 74

4 35 is an odd number. The other choices all end with even numbers.

5 The numbers are increasing by 10. The number after 44 would be 54.

6 $1.35 = 100c + 35c = 135c

7 The fourth whole number after 27 is 31 (28, 29, 30, 31).

8 6 + 15 + 5 = 6 + 20 = 26

9 When an odd and an even number are added, the result is always an odd number.

10 When rounded to the closest ten, 21 + 8 + 39 become 20 + 10 + 40, which equals 70.

11 26 + 22 = 48

12 61 is greater than (>) 57. 83 is not less than (<) 78; 18 is not greater than 61; 56 does not equal 65.

13 The totals are 30, 29, 30 and 31. 13 + 18 = 31.

14 32 + 65 = 97

15 78 – 60 = 18

16 43 + 56 = 99

17 The units (ones) must total 9. Since 5 + 3 = 8, the number in the square must be 1.

18 In the units column, 6 minus a number is 1. This means the missing number is 5.

19 First subtract $1 from $5 to get $4, then subtract 75c from the whole $4, which leaves $3.25.

20 The least number of coins is 4 (1 × $2, 1 × 50c, 1 × 20c and 1 × 5c coins).

1 C 2 B 3 2047 4 C 5 C 6 A 7 C 8 C 9 A
10 B 11 B 12 A 13 D 14 D 15 A 16 B

EXPLANATIONS

1 Three thousand and forty
= 3 × 1000 + 4 × 10
= 3 × 1000 + 0 × 100 + 4 × 10 + 0 × 1
= 3040

2 The change will be the difference between
$3 = 300 cents and $2.30 = 230 cents
Change = 300 – 230
= 70
The change is $0.70

$$\begin{array}{r} 300 \\ -\,230 \\ \hline 70 \end{array}$$

3 2 × 1000 + 4 × 10 + 7 × 1
= 2 × 1000 + 0 × 100 + 4 × 10 + 7 × 1
= 2047

4 Difference = 35 – 14
= 35 – 10 – 4
= 25 – 4
= 21
The difference is 21.

5 Sum = 23 + 52 + 10
= 85
The sum is 85.

$$\begin{array}{r} 23 \\ 52 \\ +\,10 \\ \hline 85 \end{array}$$

6 In the units column, 3 + 4 = 7.
For the tens column, 2 and 'what number' is 5?
This means the missing number is 3.

7 68 + 5 = 68 + 2 + 3
          = 70 + 3
          = 73
Jessa finished at 73.

8 The largest even number will end in a 0 or an even number; the largest is 270.

9 6042 = six thousand 0 hundreds 4 tens and two
       = six thousand and forty-two

10 We can arrange the numbers from lowest to highest: 34, 66, 136, 203. This means the largest number is 203.

11 26 − 11 − 4 = 15 − 4
             = 11
Mark had 11 cards left.

12 100 − 27 = 100 − 20 − 7
            = 80 − 7
            = 73
The answer is 73

13 Counting: 2 rows of 10 + 6
            = 2 × 10 + 6
            = 26

14 Grandpa's age = 67 + 8
               = 67 + 3 + 5
               = 70 + 5
               = 75
Grandpa is 75 years old.

15 $2 + 50c + 20c + 20c + 5c = $2 + 95c
                            = $2.95

16 The two odd numbers are 17 and 35 because they end in an odd digit
Difference = 35 − 17
           = 35 − 10 − 7
           = 25 − 7
           = 25 − 5 − 2
           = 20 − 2
           = 18
The difference is 18

NUMBER AND ALGEBRA (Test Your Skills)
Multiplication and division   Page 6

Addition

1 There are five fours, so the correct answer is 5 × 4.

2 3 × 9 = 27

3 4 × 12 = 48

4 5 × 7 = 35

5 First multiply the units: 3 × 1 = 3. Now the tens: 3 × 2 = 6. This means the answer is 63.

6 Billy's bathroom is 6 tiles wide by 5 tiles long. To find the total number of tiles required, multiply 6 × 5 = 30.

7 $7 × 4 = $28.

8 Any number multiplied by zero (0) gives a product of zero. 3 × 2 = 6 but 6 × 0 is zero.

9 This is a sequence of multiples of 3. The missing number is 12 + 3 = 15.

Division

1 24 divided by 6 equals 4 (4 × 6 = 24).

2 3 × 6 = 18

3 This question means division. 42 ÷ 7 = 6 (7 × 6 = 42).

4 30 ÷ 10 = 3 (10 × 3 = 30)

5 'Sharing' means dividing. $24 ÷ 3 = $8 (3 × $8 = $24).

6 27 ÷ 5 = 5 remainder 2. (25 + 2 = 27).

7 9 divided by 3 = 3. 6 divided by 3 = 2. Missing number is 6. (Or you can multiply 3 × 32 to find the answer.)

8 $30.00 ÷ 6 = $5 ($5 × 6 = $30).

9 Five can be taken away 9 times.
$45 - 5 - 5 - 5 - 5 - 5 - 5 - 5 - 5 - 5 = 0$.

10 Emily had half her cards left (4) after giving the other half to her sister, which means she had 8 cards at that stage. Those 8 cards were half of what she had originally, which means she started with 16 cards.
$4 \times 2 \times 2 = 16$.

NUMBER AND ALGEBRA (Real Test)
Multiplication and division   **Page 9**

---

1 D 2 D 3 B 4 A 5 C 6 C 7 D 8 B 9 D 10 D
11 9 12 D 13 A 14 D 15 B 16 C

EXPLANATIONS

1 Half of 20 is 10 and double 9 is 18
Answer $= 10 + 18$
$= 28$

2 No. of legs $= 3 \times 4 + 5 \times 2$
$= 12 + 10$
$= 22$

3 Cost $= 3 \times 80$
$= 240$
This means 240 cents, or \$2.40

4 Check each of the choices:
$13 \div 5 = 2$ with 3 remainder
$12 \div 4 = 3$ with no remainder
$17 \div 4 = 4$ with 1 remainder
$16 \div 5 = 3$ with 1 remainder
This means 13 divided by 5 has remainder 3

5 Each lot of 3 costs 60c
Now, number of 60c in \$3 $= 300 \div 60$
$= 5$
This means that we can buy 5 lots of the kiwi fruit.
Total number purchased $= 5 \times 3$
$= 15$
15 kiwi fruit can be bought

6 29 is closer to 30 than 20
47 is closer to 50 than 40
The best estimate is 30×50

7 Multiplying a whole number by 10 means we place a zero on the end of the number:
$403 \times 10 = 4030$

8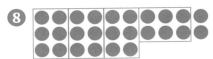

There are 2 left over

9 $6 \times 5 = 30$
There are 30 flowers altogether

10 Number of stickers $4 \times 5 = 20$
Jocelyn has 20 stickers to give to her friends

11 $6 \times$ 'what number' is 54?
The number must be 9, as $6 \times 9 = 54$
The answer is 9

12 Total time $= 7 \times 3$
$= 21$
Stops for a total of 21 minutes

13 Total number of slices $= 3 \times 8$
$= 24$
Number of slices eaten = 15
Slices remaining $= 24 - 15$
$= 24 - 14 - 1$
$= 10 - 1$
$= 9$
9 slices remaining

14 Total money $= 3 \times 50 + 2 \times 20$
$= 150 + 40$
$= 190$
Mim has 190 cents, or \$1.90

15 Share $= 66 \div 3$
$= 22$
Each nephew receives \$22

16 Change \$1.80 to 180 cents
Cost $= 180 \times 2 + 60$
$= \$4.20$
Change $= \$5.00 - \$4.20$
$= 80c$

$$\begin{array}{r} 180 \\ \times\ 2 \\ \hline 360 \end{array} \qquad \begin{array}{r} 360 \\ +\ 60 \\ \hline 420 \end{array}$$

SPELLING (Real Test)
Common misspellings   Page 11

1 a glasses b early c screws d scrub e many
f slept g filing h said

2 a pliers b spanner c hammer d screw

3 a getting b shoe c were d tried e just
f body

GRAMMAR AND PUNCTUATION (Real Test)
Types of sentences and articles   Pages 13–14

1 B 2 C 3 B 4 A 5 D 6 A 7 A 8 C 9 A 10 B
11 C 12 D 13 D 14 B 15 A 16 C 17 D 18 A

EXPLANATIONS

1 When the subject is plural (*Tim* and *Tom*) the verb must be plural (*are*).

2 Use *an* before words that start with vowels: *an insect*.

3 Molly is *the* only person. *The* is used to indicate a particular person.

4 The correct conjunction is *over*.

5 *Neither* and *nor* go together (as do *either* and *or*).

6 *Premier* and *Queensland* are proper nouns which refer to the title and need capital letters. The word *outback* is a common noun. *The Premier of Queensland toured the outback.*

7 *Keep* is the correct verb. *Kept* is past tense. 'Keept' and 'keeped' are not words.

8 This is the beginning of a new sentence. The word *There* is the correct word as it indicates a particular place.

9 The correct conjunction is *and*.

10 The correct preposition in this situation is *along*. The trees grows *along* the creek.

11 *Morning* is the particular time of the day. This refers to just one morning.

12 The reader is asked a question. The sentence must end with a question mark.

13 This is a question sentence and must end with a question mark. *Has Tony finished his meal?*

14 Harley is the owner of the bike. *Trees* and *bus* are not involved in ownership. *I saw Harley's bike under trees near the bus stop.*

15 *Left* is the correct verb. 'Leaved' and 'lefted' are not words and not the past tense of *leave*.

16 *Faster* is correct. It is used to show the difference between two different bikes. *Fastest* would only be used if comparing more than two bikes. *More fast* is incorrect.

17 This is a two-part statement. The full stop goes at the very end. *Dennis can carry the paper and Lindy will carry the mail and new CD.*

18 *Circular* is unnecessary. It is a redundant word. It carries the same meaning as *ring*. A *ring* in this context is *circular*.

READING (Test Your Skills)
Understanding narratives   Page 15

The Heron and the Crab

1 The story is part of a fable. A fable is usually a story involving animals that has a lesson or warning for the readers. It is not from a true adventure, because animals can't speak, so the extract cannot be true. It is not from a mystery novel. A legend is usually a story about supernatural beings in an earlier age e.g. ancient stories of mythical figures (such as Hercules, etc), usually showing how or why something happened, so the extract is not from a legend.

2 'Grab' is the best word as it describes a quick action to get hold of something. 'Trap' is usually a slower process. 'Snap' is more like a sudden shutting or breaking. 'Hold' suggests that the prey has already been snatched.

3 The heron is being sneaky or tricky. He has a secret plan and he has lied. He is only pretending to be friendly and helpful. He is not at all confused—it is the crab and fish who are confused by his story.

4 The heron was pretending to be worried. The story that the villagers were about to net the pond was a lie. The fish knew the heron was their enemy. The crab was not trying to catch fish.

5 The heron said the villagers could be arriving in a few days.

6 The fish should be most afraid of the heron, their enemy. The story about the village fishermen was made up by the heron.

READING (Real Test)
Understanding narratives   Page 16

Simon's Solution

1 B   2 C   3 C   4 A   5 C   6 A   7 D

EXPLANATIONS

1 Simon and his father were out in the fields of a farm looking at their crop of corn. They couldn't have been in a barn because Simon's father looked up at the sky to see the birds.

2 'Grim' means stern or harsh. Simon's father may have been annoyed with the crows and getting impatient, but these do not have the same meaning as 'grim'. 'Grime' has something to do with being dirty.

3 Simon would find the pieces he wanted in the shed.

4 Earlier Simon had been helping his father to fix a fence.

5 The extract tells the reader it was school holidays, which is why Simon was able to help his father. Simon had a made a bookcase some time ago for his mother.

6 Simon was excited. The word 'declared' gives the idea that he was excited with his idea and he liked making things.

7 Simon tells his father that he made his mother a bookcase. His father drove the tractor, there is no mention of him going to help his mother, and they have not been chasing birds.

READING (Real Test)
Understanding narratives   Page 17

Fearless Brian

1 D   2 C   3 B   4 A   5 A   6 (3, 4, 1, 2)   7 B

EXPLANATIONS

1 Brian might have thought he was saving a dolphin but he was actually daydreaming. His daydreams were about saving a dolphin. He wasn't doing homework. ✓

2 There were four people in the family: mother, father, sister (Devona) and Brian himself.

3 She was most likely becoming frustrated as Brian had to be reminded about his homework and coming to dinner. She would not be afraid of Brian's daydreaming, and she was certainly not excited or delighted by his daydream bravery.

4 Brian was behaving like a real lion tamer. He would use the chair for safety and defence. He wouldn't sit on it while doing his act. There is no reason to climb onto it.

5 Brian though he was brave because his name meant 'strong and powerful'. His mother wasn't interested in him doing dangerous things—just his homework.

6 The correct order of events is (3, 4, 1, 2).

7 A swishing sound is like a soft or whispering breeze. Sausages sizzling, flies buzzing or a stream gushing would be too noisy.

READING (Real Test)
Understanding narratives   Page 18

Fancy Dress Party

1 B **2** B **3** C **4** A **5** B **6** D
EXPLANATIONS

1 We are told Amanda always had the 'best prizes'.

2 It is most likely the party's theme was red because Amanda's last name was 'Redding'.

3 Dad suggested, as a joke, that Tim could go to the party as a red robin.

4 By Thursday Tim would have been feeling worried because his family couldn't come up with an idea for a costume. He should have been excited, but the extract indicates that he is worried.

5 The word 'summoned' has a similar meaning to ordered, but it is most likely Amanda used the word in place of 'invited', because she really wanted people to come to her party. (The key is in the use of the word 'fun' in the question.)

6 Tim found his invitation in the letterbox, so it is most likely to have been delivered by mail.

READING (Real Test)
Understanding narratives   Page 19

Puppets

1 B **2** C **3** written response **4** D **5** A **6** D **7** A
EXPLANATIONS

1 The information would not be in a manual, which shows how things work. It is not part of a story or a novel. It is unlikely to be in sports magazine. It would most likely be in a travel book for people who want to visit Java in Indonesia.

2 To do something 'frequently' means to do it over and over again, or very often.

3 Possible answer:
According to the text, the puppeteer also 'directs the gamalan orchestra which sits behind him and plays music during the performance'.

4 The thin puppets are made from animal hides. 'Hide' is another word for an animal skin. The text says they are made from goat or buffalo skin.

5 A dalang is a puppeteer who makes the puppets move with rods.

6 The rods are made from strips of animal horn.

7 Javanese puppet plays are shadow plays. The puppets have lights behind them which cast shadows that the audience can see. We are told in the text that the dalang makes up the dialogue for the puppets, which means that they have speaking parts. The puppets are operated by a single puppeteer. The puppets are not on strings—they are on rods.

WRITING (Real Test)
Persuasive text 1   Page 24

Tick each correct point.
Read the student's work through once to get an overall view of their response.

Focus on general points
☑ Did it make sense?
☑ Did it flow? Were the arguments logical and relevant?
☐ Did the opinions expressed arouse any feelings/reactions?
☑ Was the body of the writing mainly in the third person?
☑ Did you want to read on to understand/ appreciate the writer's point of view?
☐ Were the arguments convincing?
☑ Has the writer been assertive (e.g. the use of *is* rather than a less definite term)?

☑ Was the handwriting readable?
☑ Was the writing style suitable for a persuasive text (objective; not casual or dismissive)?

Now focus on the detail. Read each of the following points and find out whether the student's work has these features.

Focus on content
☑ Did the opening sentence(s) focus on the topic?
☑ Was the writer's point of view established early in the writing?
☐ Did the writer include any evidence to support his or her opinion?
☐ Did the writer include information relevant to his or her experiences?
☑ Were the points/arguments raised by the writer easy to follow?
☑ Did the writing follow the format with an introduction, the body of the text and a conclusion?
☐ Were personal opinions included?
☑ Was the concluding paragraph relevant to the topic?

Focus on structure, vocabulary, grammar, spelling, punctuation
☑ Was there a variety of sentence lengths, types and beginnings?
☐ Was a new paragraph started for each additional argument or point?
☐ Has the writer used any similes (e.g. *as clear as crystal*) to stress a point raised?
☑ Did the writer avoid approximations such as *probably, perhaps* and *maybe*?
☐ Did the writer use such phrases as *I know …* and *It is important to …*?
☑ Did the writer refer to the question in the points raised (A good way to do this is to use the key words from the question or the introduction.)?
☐ Has the writer used any less common words correctly?
☐ Was indirect speech used correctly?
☐ Were adjectives used to improve descriptions (e.g. *expensive* buildings)?
☐ Were adverbs used effectively (e.g. *firstly*)?
☑ Were capital letters used correctly?

☑ Was punctuation used correctly?
☐ Was the spelling of words correct? *nearly all.*

Marker's suggestions (optional)

WRITING (Real Test)
Persuasive text 2   Page 25

Tick each correct point.
Read the student's work through once to get an overall view of their response.

Focus on general points
☐ Did it make sense?
☐ Did it flow? Were the arguments logical and relevant?
☐ Did the opinions expressed arouse any feelings/reactions?
☐ Was the body of the writing mainly in the third person?
☐ Did you want to read on to understand/ appreciate the writer's point of view? Were the arguments convincing?
☐ Has the writer been assertive (e.g. the use of *is* rather than a less definite term)?
☐ Was the handwriting readable?
☐ Was the writing style suitable for a persuasive text (objective; not casual or dismissive)?

Now focus on the detail. Read each of the following points and find out whether the student's work has these features.

Focus on content
☐ Did the opening sentence(s) focus on the topic?
☐ Was the writer's point of view established early in the writing?
☐ Did the writer include any evidence to support his or her opinion?
☐ Did the writer include information relevant to his or her experiences?
☐ Were the points/arguments raised by the writer easy to follow?

☐ Did the writing follow the format with an introduction, the body of the text and a conclusion?

☐ Were personal opinions included?

☐ Was the concluding paragraph relevant to the topic?

Focus on structure, vocabulary, grammar, spelling, punctuation

☐ Was there a variety of sentence lengths, types and beginnings?

☐ Was a new paragraph started for each additional argument or point?

☐ Has the writer used any similes (e.g. *as clear as crystal*) to stress a point raised?

☐ Did the writer avoid approximations such as *probably, perhaps* and *maybe*?

☐ Did the writer use such phrases as *I know …* and *It is important to …*?

☐ Did the writer refer to the question in the points raised (A good way to do this is to use the key words from the question or the introduction.)?

☐ Has the writer used any less common words correctly?

☐ Was indirect speech used correctly?

☐ Were adjectives used to improve descriptions (e.g. *expensive* buildings)?

☐ Were adverbs used effectively (e.g. *firstly*)?

☐ Were capital letters used correctly?

☐ Was punctuation used correctly?

☐ Was the spelling of words correct?

Marker's suggestions (optional)

WEEK 2

> **NUMBER AND ALGEBRA/MEASUREMENT AND GEOMETRY (Test Your Skills)**
> *Fractions, percentages and time*   **Page 28**

Fractions and percentages

1 There are three thirds in one whole. Wholes are named after the number of parts in the whole, e.g. 1 whole is the same as five fifths, six sixths, etc.

2 11 + 11 = 22. 11 is half of 22.

3 Half of 7 is $3\frac{1}{2}$. Remember that half of 6 is 3, and half of 1 more is $\frac{1}{2}$ $\left(\text{total } 3\frac{1}{2}\right)$.

4 1 half = 2 quarters $\left(\frac{1}{2} = \frac{2}{4}\right)$. $\frac{2}{4}$ plus another quarter = $\frac{3}{4}$

5 There are 10 tenths in 1 whole, so there are 20 tenths in 2 wholes.

6 There are 2 halves in 1 whole so 3 halves must be $1\frac{1}{2}$.

7 Sandy got half of her words right. She got 50% because 50% is half of 100%.

8 The shape has five parts. Three of the five are not shaded, so $\frac{3}{5}$ is not shaded.

9 Full marks is the same as 100%. Levi got 75%. 100% − 75% = 25% so Levi needed another 25% for full marks.

10 $\frac{3}{4}$ is greater than (>) $\frac{1}{4}$. $\frac{1}{5}$ is not greater than $\frac{1}{2}$; $\frac{1}{2}$ is not less than $\frac{1}{10}$; $\frac{1}{3}$ is not less than $\frac{1}{10}$.

Time

1 30 minutes (or half an hour) after 4:15 is 4:45, which can also be expressed as quarter to 5.

2 1 week = 7 days, so 2 weeks = 7 + 7 = 14 days.

3 The fifth month after April: May (1) June (2) July (3) August (4) and September (5). The answer is September.

Check Your Answers

4 There were 14 years until her birthday in 2006 (2006 − 1992 = 14).

5 The time is quarter to two (1:45). The minute hand has gone three quarters of the hourly circuit, and has only one quarter to go.

6 1200 hours is midday, so 1300 hours will be 1 o'clock in the afternoon, or 1 pm.

7 Winter is June (30 days), July (31 days) and August (31 days), giving a total of 92 days.

8 Mrs Buddle lived 13 years after 1981. 1981 + 13 = 1994.

9 2:40 is 40 minutes after 2 o'clock, or 20 minutes to 3.

NUMBER AND ALGEBRA/MEASUREMENT AND GEOMETRY (Real Test)
Fractions, percentages and time   Page 31

1 D **2** B **3** C **4** C **5** D **6** A **7** C **8** C **9** A **10** C
11 B **12** C **13** B **14** A **15** B **16** A
EXPLANATIONS

1 Halfway between 3 and 4 is $3\frac{1}{2}$

2 One quarter of 12 = 12 ÷ 4
                                    = 3

3 We can compare the fractions in a diagram:

whole							
halves							
thirds							
quarters							
eighths							

The largest fraction is one half.

4 There are 9 small squares and 5 squares are shaded. This means $\frac{5}{9}$ of the shape.

5 There are 14 hearts, and 8 are shaded.

This means $\frac{8}{14}$ which is the same as $\frac{4}{7}$.

6 Full marks is 100%.
Difference = 100 − 82
              = 100 − 80 − 2
              = 20 − 2
              = 18
This means 18% more is needed.

7 Total time = 20 × 5
              = 100
This means 100 minutes.
As 60 minutes = 1 hour, and
        100 = 60 + 40,
she exercises for 1 hour 40 minutes

8 Time is a quarter to 4 which is 3:45

9 Tuesday 16th June + 7 days = 23rd June
Now we need 4 more days:
Tuesday 23rd + 4 days = Saturday 27th
This means 27th June is Saturday.

10 From 4:20, we add 1 hour 30 minutes:
This means 4:20 + 1 hr + 30 min
              = 5:20 + 30 min
              = 5:50
The movie finishes at 5:50 pm.

11 We need to find the amount of time between 11:30 am to 1:00 pm. From 11:30 am to 12:00 is 30 minutes and 12:00 to 1:00 is 1 hour. This means 1 hour 30 minutes.

12 Present time = 4:10
Time training starts = 4:10 + 5 min
                        = 4:15
Time training finishes = 4:15 + 1 hour
                          = 5:15
Training finishes at 5:15 pm.

13 As May has 31 days, there are 7 days from 24th May to end of May.
As 7 + 5 = 12, this leaves another 5 days in June.
Dinh's birthday is on 5th June.

14 Half an hour = 30 minutes
Number of pages = 30 ÷ 2
                    = 15
Phoebe reads 15 pages.

15 Time difference = 3:55 pm − 3:15 pm
                   = 55 − 15
                   = 40
Show runs for 40 minutes

16 Count forward 25 from 1998.
Year = 1998 + 25
       = 1998 + 2 + 23
       = 2000 + 23
       = 2023
Jackson will be 25 in 2023

**MEASUREMENT AND GEOMETRY
(Test Your Skills)
*2D shapes, 3D shapes and position*** Page 32

2D shapes

1 All these shapes are quadrilaterals (four-sided shapes). A rectangle is a quadrilateral with four sides, and has opposite sides parallel. All four angles are right angles. Shape B is the only one with these features.

2 Parallel lines are straight lines that never meet. ⬜ has parallel lines.

3 Right angles are often called 'square' angles.

4 Hexagons have 6 sides.

5 A perpendicular line is at 90° (at a right angle) to a given line.

6 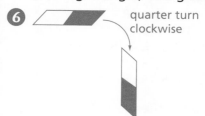 quarter turn clockwise

3D shapes

1 This shape is a cylinder. All the other shapes have flat faces and straight edges.

2 There are 9 blocks in each of the 2 rows, giving a total of 18.

3 When folded, the net will make a rectangular prism.

4 The little block is sitting on the front edge of the larger block.

5 A tennis ball is most like a sphere shape. It looks like a circle when you draw it on paper, but its 3D shape is a sphere.

6 Imagine looking down on this block from above. When the block is cut straight through as shown, the cut faces will be the same shape as the top—a rectangle.

**MEASUREMENT AND GEOMETRY
(Real Test)
*2D shapes, 3D shapes and position*** Page 35

1 D **2** B **3** B **4** D **5** C **6** C **7** C **8** D **9** D **10** A
11 A **12** B **13** B **14** A **15** C **16** C
EXPLANATIONS

1 trapezium

2 M ⋮ M

3 An octagon has 8 sides:

4 There are 4 lines of symmetry:

5 O does not have any parallel lines

6 There are 5 rectangles in the shape.

7 The solid is a rectangular prism which has 6 faces.

8 The shape is a cylinder

9 A cube has 4 + 4 + 4 = 12 edges.

10 The view from the top is a rectangle and the edges appear as lines.

11 There are 3 rectangles.

12 The shape would be a rectangle.

13 The tin is in the shape of a cylinder

14 From Z, the direction of the bookshop is between south and east. This means south east.

15 Laura is on bottom row, so that second from the right on top row is Sam.

16 P is in column B, row 3.
This means that P is at B3.

SPELLING (Real Test)
Common misspellings **Page 37**

1 a loaf b broom c brown d brick e comb
f barked g smiling h cleaner

2 a handle b steel c front d wheel

3 a whales b much c beak d They e to
f making

GRAMMAR AND PUNCTUATION (Real Test)
Types of nouns and adjectives **Pages 39–40**

1 B 2 C 3 A 4 C 5 B 6 A 7 A 8 D 9 B 10 D
11 C 12 A 13 D 14 D 15 B 16 B 17 C 18 C

EXPLANATIONS

1 When the subject is singular (*train*) the verb must be singular (*stops*).

2 *Caught* is the correct verb. 'Catched' and 'caughted' are not words and not the past tense of *catch*.

3 Use *oldest* when comparing more than two people or things. There are more than

two people in the group. Use *older* when comparing two people or things.

4 The opposite of *hot* is *cold*.

5 The correct conjunction is *because*. It gives the reason for the reward.

6 Mr Hughes will teach and the pupils will learn. *Taught* is past tense. 'Teached' is not a word.

7 Both *France* and their nationality (*French*) are proper nouns and have capital letters. *People* is a common noun.

8 *Italy* is a proper noun. It begins with a capital *I*. It is the last word in a question sentence so it is followed by a question mark.

9 The word *their*, showing ownership (of the coffee) is the correct word. This is not the beginning of a new sentence.

10 The word *of* is correct. *Of* is used between nouns. 'Ov' is not a word.

11 The correct preposition in this situation is *In*. It is the beginning of a new sentence.

12 The subject is plural (*islands*) and must have a plural verb (*are*).

13 The word *water* is the last word in a statement which has to have a full stop.

14 The proper nouns are *Friday* and *Belmont Park*. All other nouns are common nouns.

15 Use *much* to describe things that cannot be counted (*sand*).

16 There are two sentences in this exercise. The second statement sentence begins with *I*. *How far can you count? I can count by tens to one hundred.*

17 There is one stranger who owns a pair of shoes. *Shoes*, *holes* and *laces* are common plural nouns which don't involve ownership. *The stranger's shoes were full of holes and without laces.*

18 The word *up* is unnecessary. Something being lifted must by definition come up from a lower position. No meaning is lost by omitting *up*.

READING (Test Your Skills)
Interpreting visual texts Page 41

Cartoon

1 The donkeys are trying to reach two separate piles of hay. The rope is not long enough for the donkeys to go in opposite directions.

2 The question mark indicates that the donkeys have a problem and need to solve it. They are wondering what to do.

3 Frame 5 shows both donkeys eating the hay, and Frame 6 shows that the pile has gone.

4 The donkeys are most likely feeling happy and contented. Their tails are wagging.

5 Both donkeys are sniffing the hay (food). This fits better with the sequence of events than sneezing, shouting (they are donkeys!) or snuffling (they are not close enough to the hay to 'snuffle' it).

6 The most obvious lesson the illustrations show is 'Sharing is better than arguing' or 'Cooperation is better than competition'. When the donkeys stop going in opposite directions and share their hay, they reap the benefits. 'Two heads are better than one' does not quite fit, as the illustration is more about the benefits of sharing than of brain power!

READING (Real Test)
Interpreting visual texts Page 42

Play, play, play!
1 C 2 A 3 B 4 B 5 C 6 A 7 D

EXPLANATIONS

1 Lessons are provided for piano, guitar, drums and school recorder. Singing lessons are not 'instrument' lessons.

2 Appropriate means 'suitable'.

3 The flier is meant to make lessons enjoyable or fun. There is no indication of them being 'cheap' or 'private', and the design of the flier and the word 'fun' indicates that it can be enjoyable.

4 The music notes would show people that the flier is about playing music. The notes would not indicate that learning would be easy, and we would assume that the instructor knows music.

5 Before commencing lessons students should contact the studio for a 'free trial lesson'. There is no requirement to be able to read music, and the age of the student is not relevant.

6 Popular music is enjoyed by most people , that's why it's called 'popular'. It's not just teenagers who listen to it!

7 This is an exaggeration to show how easy it is for people of any age to learn.

READING (Test Your Skills)
Understanding poetry Page 43

My Cat

1 This poem describes a pet cat from the owner's point of view. There is no story to be told and no problems to be explored. It covers more than one 'scene'.

2 'Waste' rhymes with 'taste'.

3 The pet owner is caring. She/he feeds the cat and plays with it. She/he is not lazy when it comes to caring for the cat. Caring for the cat doesn't bother her/him.

4 A fluffy cat would be soft and cuddly. Fluffy cats are not usually heavy though they look larger than they are. They are not smooth to pat, or shiny.

5 The poet tells us that 'Before she eats she smells her meat'.

6 The cat gets excited when the owner comes home because it is getting close to tea time. The cat eats chicken wings so we can assume she likes them. She is not messy as she licks the bowl clean. The cat looks like a cotton ball—the poet does not say that the cat plays with them.

READING (Real Test)
Understanding poetry   Page 44

Clean Your Room!

1 B **2** A **3** D **4** B **5** A **6** C **7** (2, 1, 4, 3)

EXPLANATIONS

1 The poem looks at the problem Katie has in keeping her room tidy. It doesn't tell a story. Katie and her mother have a different attitude to housework.

2 The word 'cleared' in the poem means the dishes are collected to be put in the sink or dishwasher to be washed.

3 Katie feels it is useless to tidy her room because 'It will only get dirty again!'.

4 Katie expects her mother to come in and inspect her room to see that it is tidy: 'I know once it's clean,/ And Mum's been in and seen …'

5 The last line suggests that Katie feels that tidying her room has no purpose and is pointless. Katie's mother is probably not being unfair in expecting her to keep her room tidy; Katie does not seem lazy; and the poem is not really saying that keeping a house tidy is important.

6 The poem suggests Katie prefers reading. She is told to put her book away, and she only folds her T-shirts because her mother has told her to.

7 Carefully study the poem to see the order in which Katie's mother does her work: (2, 1, 4, 3).

READING (Real Test)
Understanding poetry   Page 45

Quiet please!

1 A **2** D **3** C **4** A **5** written response **6** C **7** B

EXPLANATIONS

1 The action in the poem takes place in a home. It mentions a bedroom, children's toys and a TV.

2 The narrator of the poem is most likely the baby's older brother or sister. The narrator has toys and lives in the house.

3 The narrator feels unfairly treated. This is shown by the lines 'How come she's the only one/Allowed to make a noise?', meaning that the baby is 'allowed' to cry but everyone else has to keep quiet.

4 The exclamation mark shows that the words are a command or an order. We don't know if anyone else is being particularly noisy, or if the baby is crying— and it is not mentioned that anyone has entered the baby's room.

5 Possible answer:
'Asleep' rhymes with 'creep'.

6 The baby has just gone to sleep. This information is contained in the line, 'She's only just asleep'.

7 Playing Nintendo is 'out of bounds', meaning that it's banned. The TV can be watched but it is turned down low. To move around the house people have to tip-toe. People can go near the baby's room but they must 'creep'.

Page 47

WRITING (Real Test)
Recount 1

Tick each correct point.
Read the student's work through once to get an overall view of their response.

Focus on general points
- ☐ Did it make sense?
- ☐ Did it flow?
- ☐ Did the events arouse any feeling?
- ☐ Did you want to read on? (Were the events interesting?)
- ☐ Was the handwriting readable?

Now focus on the detail. Read each of the following points and find out whether the student's work has these features.

Focus on content
- ☐ Did the opening sentence(s) introduce the subject of the recount?
- ☐ Was the setting established, i.e. when and where the action took place?
- ☐ Was the reader told when the action takes place?
- ☐ Was it apparent who the main characters(s) is/are?
- ☐ Have personal pronouns been used? (e.g. *I, we, our*)
- ☐ Were the events recorded in chronological (time) order?
- ☐ Was the recount in past tense?
- ☐ Did the writing include some personal comments on the events? (e.g. *surprised, thrilled*)
- ☐ Did descriptions make reference to any of the senses? (e.g. *wet rocks, salty air*)
- ☐ Were interesting details included?
- ☐ Did the conclusion have a satisfactory summing-up comment?

Focus on structure, vocabulary, grammar, spelling, punctuation

- ☐ Was there a variation in sentence length and beginnings?
- ☐ Was there a new paragraph started for changes in time, place or action?
- ☐ Were subheadings used? (optional)
- ☐ Were adjectives used to improve descriptions? (e.g. *smelly* bait)
- ☐ Were adverbs used to make 'actions' more interesting? (e.g. *yelled loudly*)
- ☐ Were adverbs used for time changes? (e.g. *later, soon, then*)
- ☐ Were capital letters where they should have been?
- ☐ Was punctuation correct?
- ☐ Was the spelling of words correct?

Marker's suggestions (optional)

WRITING (Real Test)
Recount 2

Page 48

Tick each correct point.
Read the student's work through once to get an overall view of their response.

Focus on general points
- ☐ Did it make sense?
- ☐ Did it flow?
- ☐ Did the events arouse any feeling?
- ☐ Did you want to read on? (Were the events interesting?)
- ☐ Was the handwriting readable?

Now focus on the detail. Read each of the following points and find out whether the student's work has these features.

Focus on content
- ☐ Did the opening sentence(s) introduce the subject of the recount?
- ☐ Was the setting established, i.e. when and where the action took place?
- ☐ Was the reader told when the action takes place?
- ☐ Was it apparent who the main characters(s) is/are?
- ☐ Have personal pronouns been used (e.g. *I, we, our*)?
- ☐ Were the events recorded in chronological (time) order?
- ☐ Was the recount in past tense?
- ☐ Did the writing include some personal comments on the events? (e.g. *feeling cold, disappointed*)

☐ Did descriptions make reference to any of the senses? (e.g. *loud commentary, blue water*)

☐ Were interesting details included?

☐ Did the conclusion have a satisfactory summing-up comment?

Focus on structure, vocabulary, grammar, spelling, punctuation

☐ Was there a variation in sentence length and beginnings?

☐ Was there a new paragraph started for changes in time, place or action?

☐ Were subheadings used? (optional)

☐ Were adjectives used to improve descriptions? (e.g. <u>frozen</u> ground)

☐ Were adverbs used to make 'actions' more interesting? (e.g. swam <u>strongly</u>)

☐ Were adverbs used for time changes? (e.g. *later, soon, then*)

☐ Were capital letters where they should have been?

☐ Was punctuation correct?

☐ Was the spelling of words correct?

Marker's suggestions (optional)

WEEK 3

MEASUREMENT AND GEOMETRY
(Test Your Skills)
Length, mass and capacity   Page 50

Length

❶ The measurement is metres. Millimetres and centimetres are too small. Kilometres are too long.

❷ The top of an average table is about 70 cm from the floor. The seat of a chair is about 40 cm from the floor.

❸ There are 100 centimetres in 1 metre, so for 2.5 (two and a half) metres:
$100 \times 2\frac{1}{2} = 250$. There are 250 cm in 2.5 m.

❹ A square has four sides of equal length. 4 × 5 cm = 20 cm.

❺ There are two sides of 9 cm and two sides of 6 cm. (2 × 9 cm) + (2 × 6 cm) = 30 cm.

❻ The line has a slight wave in it, making it around 8 cm.

❼ The best way to measure the width of a bedroom would be to use a tape measure. Trundle wheels and paces would not be accurate. A classroom ruler would involve many small measurements.

❽ A common bucket would have a capacity of about 10 litres (five 2 L bottles of soft drink).

❾ Michael lives 3 km from school. Each day he would travel 2 × 3 km = 6 km (to school and back). There are 5 school days in most weeks, so 5 × 6 km = 30 km.

Mass and capacity

❶ Litres are used to measure liquids. Milligrams are too small and kilograms are too large for a tub of margarine. We use grams.

❷ There are 1000 grams in a kilogram, so 1000 g – 250 g = 750 g.

❸ The pointer on the scales is just above 75 kg. It is measuring about 78 kg.

❹ There are 1000 mL in a litre, so the mass would be 1000 × 1 g = 1000 g = 1 kg.

❺ There are 1000 grams in a kilogram, so for 2.5 (two and a half) kilograms: 1000 × 2.5 = 2500. There are 2500 g in 2.5 kg.

❻ An egg would have a mass of about 50 g. The mass of each egg is often shown on egg cartons—anywhere from 50 g to 80 g per egg. A postcard would be lighter, while a cricket ball and a tub of ice-cream would be heavier than 50 g.

7 The student with the heaviest mass is Leanne (61 kg). The student with the lightest mass is Sammy (43 kg).
61 kg – 43 kg = 18 kg.

MEASUREMENT AND GEOMETRY (Real Test)
Length, mass and capacity   Page 52

1 D 2 A 3 D 4 C 5 A 6 C 7 B 8 B 9 A 10 B
11 D 12 A 13 B 14 C 15 D 16 B

EXPLANATIONS

1 Deeane is the tallest person.

2 The mass of a pen is closest to 10 grams

3 Distance = 6 + 2 + 6 + 2
         = 16
Distance is 16 units

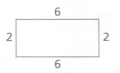

4 Distance = 600 × 3
         = 1800
She ran 1800 metres

5 As 1 metre = 100 cm, we need to divide 100 by 20.
 Number of handspans = 100 ÷ 20
                        = 5
Harold used 5 handspans.

6

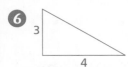

We can see that the triangle's shorter sides are 3 units and 4 units. The longer side appears to be about 5 units. The perimeter would be about 3 + 4 + 5 = 12 units

7 The book is about 20 cm high.

8 The tallest doll is 57 cm and the shortest is 39 cm.
Difference = 57 – 39
            = 57 – 40 + 1
            = 17 + 1
            = 18
The difference is 18 cm.

9 The mass of a truck would be measured in tonnes.

10 Now, take one ▮ off both sides so that we can see ▮▮ = ⬭

11 Rearranging the four choices from lightest to heaviest: 399 g, 650 g, 940 g, 1200 g. This means the lightest pumpkin has a mass of 399 g.

12 Combined mass = 62, Jack's mass = 38.
Mass of Jill = Combined mass – Jack's mass
                = 62 – 38
                = 62 – 30 – 8
                = 32 – 8
                = 24
Jill has a mass of 24 kg

13 1 litre = 1000 millilitres
Remaining custard = 1000 – 320
                    = 1000 – 300 – 20
                    = 700 – 20
                    = 680
There are 680 mL remaining in the carton

14 As there are 100 cm in a metre, then 1 metre 50 centimetres is 150 centimetres

15 The petrol tank shows half full. If 30 litres fills the tank, then the tank will have 60 litres when full.
The tank holds 60 litres

16 1 cup holds $\frac{1}{2}$ litre
This means 2 cups holds $2 \times \frac{1}{2} = 1$ litre; and, 4 cups holds 2 × 1 = 2 litres.
The four cups will hold 2 litres.

MEASUREMENT AND GEOMETRY
(Test Your Skills)
Area and volume   Page 53

1 There are three rows of eight blocks (3 × 8 = 24).

2 7 squares × 1 square metre each = 7 square metres. The space between the squares is not included in the area.

3 Each row has $4\frac{1}{2}$ bricks. $4 \times 4\frac{1}{2} = 18$.

4 Four centicubes will fit across the bottom of the width of the box. The box can take 4 blocks high and has a depth of 4 blocks. $4 \times 4 \times 4 = 64$.

5 Each square is 1 square centimetre (cm^2). Shape D has the most squares (7), so it has the greatest area.

6 A golf course is much larger than any of the other three playing areas.

7 Volume has nothing to do with mass (weight). In order of volume from smallest to largest, they are: cherry, ping-pong ball, cricket ball, blown-up balloon.

8 The green tiles fill a space of 3 tiles by 3 tiles, so $3 \times 3 = 9$.

9 The order of smallest to largest would be bus ticket, title page of a paperback book, road STOP sign, tablecloth.

10 The stack has 2 rows of 9 blocks: $(2 \times 9 = 18)$

MEASUREMENT AND GEOMETRY (Real Test)
Area and volume   Page 55

1 B 2 B 3 A 4 D 5 C 6 A 7 B 8 D 9 C 10 4
11 D 12 A 13 9 14 A 15 C 16 B

EXPLANATIONS

1

Area = 4 × 2
= 8
Area is 8 square units.

2 The shape with the largest area is the largest rectangle.

3 We need to divide 120 by 20:
Number of squares = 120 ÷ 20
= 12 ÷ 2
= 6
This means 6 squares are needed.

4 As 2 triangles cover each square we need to multiply 6 by 2:
Number of triangles = 6 × 2
= 12
12 triangles are needed.

5 The football field would have the greatest area.

6 By counting, the shape has 10 squares. This means the area is 10 square units.

7 There are 6 squares in each row. To find the number of rows, we divide 18 by 6.
Number of rows = 18 ÷ 6
= 3
There are 3 rows of squares.

8 As there are 9 boxes in each carton, to find the total boxes we multiply 9 by 6.
No. of boxes = 9 × 6
= 54
There are 54 boxes.

9 The object with the smallest volume is a marble.

10 A total of 6 stickers is needed to cover the grid. As there are already 2, we need another 4 stickers.

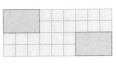

11 We count 9 small cubes. This means the volume is 9 cubic units.

12 The rectangle covers 4 small squares. This means the area is 4 square units.

13 The square covers 9 small squares. This means the area is 9 square units

14 An estimate is a guess:
We can count 2 whole squares within the triangle, and then some part squares in the rest of the triangle. This means that 4 square units would be the best estimate.

15 To find the total volume, we multiply 12 by 3:
Total volume = 12 × 3
= 36
The volume is 36 cubic centimetres.

16 By counting the squares (or 8 × 3), there are 24 squares in the shape. Half of the squares is 12. Kahli has already shaded 10 squares, so she needs to shade another 2 squares.

SPELLING (Real Test)
Common misspellings   Page 57

1 a hungry b holiday c caught d centre
e died f money g ladies h sorry

2 a main b panel c address d knob

3 a bones b strange c after d built e of
f from

GRAMMAR AND PUNCTUATION (Real Test)
Commas, verbs, tense and
'agreement'   Pages 59–60

1 C 2 C 3 C 4 A 5 D 6 A 7 C 8 B 9 D 10 B
11 C 12 D 13 A 14 B 15 C 16 A 17 B 18 D

EXPLANATIONS

1 Use *were* when talking about more than one person or thing.

2 Use *an* before words that start with vowels: *an orange sports car.*

3 *Will clean* is correct. The car cleaning will happen later—in the future.

4 The verb is *has*. Verbs tell readers about something a person, animal, force of nature or thing can do or has done. Bruce *has* an idea. Most verbs describe an action or behaviour.

5 The correct preposition in this situation is *under.*

6 The correct verb is *crept*. 'Creeped' and 'creped' are not words and not the past tense of *creep.*

7 Two commas are required. No comma is needed before *and. Martin invited Jake, Leo, Mark and Graham to his party.*

8 Uncle has a capital *U* as it is a title for Jack. No punctuation is required.

9 The correct possessive pronoun is *his. He's* is short for *he is.*

10 This is not the beginning of a new sentence. The word *their*, showing ownership, is the correct word.

11 *Perry* is a proper noun and has a capital *P*. There is no comma after *Perry* as the word *and* separates *Perry* from *Justine.*

12 When referring to people, use the personal pronoun *who.*

13 The word *circus* is a common noun at the end of a question sentence.

14 *Down* is unnecessary. It is a redundant word. It carries the same meaning as *fell from the tree*. A *fall* from a tree will always be *down.*

15 *Can't* is short for *cannot*. This sentence is a statement. A comma is not required before *or.*

16 *Worse* is correct. It is used to show the difference between two different times (last night and later). 'Worser' is not a word.

17 The comma is used to separate items in a list. *And* separates the last two items. *Later in the day we played cricket, volley ball and had a game of rounders.*

18 The comma is used to separate items in a list. *Or* separates the last two items. *Will we put oranges, apples or lemons in the basket?*

READING (Test Your Skills)
Understanding recounts   Page 61

My Diary

1 Penny is an actor. She works in a 'studio' and puts on her 'wardrobe' (costume) before 'shooting' begins. Mr Davis drives the taxi, and Penny writes in her diary (but does not do it for a job). 'Shooting' is the word she uses for 'filming'.

2 Penny wanted to stay in bed because it was 'dark and cold'—so she could stay warm by staying in bed. Penny had received her 'call' information the day before. She seems happy to go to work, and there's no indication that the alarm went off too early.

3 Penny wanted to write in her diary while riding in the taxi.

4 The answer to this question is in the extract: 'filming (or "shooting" as they say)'.

5 Penny gets her call sheet for the next day before she leaves work each day. She already has it when she leaves for the studio in the morning.

6 The correct sequence is: she hears her alarm; she starts the taxi ride; she begins writing; she puts on her 'wardrobe'. She is already in the taxi when she starts writing.

READING (Real Test)
Understanding recounts   Page 62

Before Computers

1 D 2 C 3 B 4 A 5 C 6 D

EXPLANATIONS

1 The main idea in this extract is to show how the numbers we use have changed over a long period of time. We are not told if people are smarter now or in earlier times. The other two choices are false.

2 Tally marks are most like a simple line or stroke.

3 The number shown is a digital number which would be seen on a digital watch.

4 Nowadays, most numbers used across the world look 'much the same'. The extract gives an example after the words 'most of the world's numbers look like this'. If they look much the same then they cannot be very different. Numbers no longer look like tally marks.

5 'Invented' means to make something totally new or create it. 'Produced' simply means to make (or grow). 'Found' suggests recovering something that has been lost. 'Solved' usually means 'worked out', especially a problem.

6 The best title would be 'How Numbers Continue to Change'. The other three choices are either obviously wrong or only cover a small section of the extract.

READING (Test Your Skills)
Understanding explanations   Page 63

Great Dinosaurs

1 'Habitat' is closest in meaning to 'environment'. 'Setting' relates to the background (often in films or books). Neighbourhood is more to do with people.

2 The Ankylosaurus had a mass (weight) of about 3–4 tonnes. It was the lightest dinosaur of the four.

3 The Brachiosaurus had a habitat of 'forests near lakes'.

4 The Tyrannosaurus lived in Asia and North America.

5 The diagrams show how large the dinosaurs were in relation to the size of people. People did not live during the time of the dinosaurs, so dinosaurs could not eat them and scientists could not study dinosaurs.

6 This information would be found in a reference book. A manual is used to explain how something works (such as a car or a computer). Stories are not presented using facts in this way. A diary is a personal recount of events in a person's life.

Pandas

1 B 2 B 3 D 4 A 5 C 6 B 7 D

EXPLANATIONS

1 The purpose of the extract is to explain why pandas are in danger of dying out. Their eating habits and natural enemies are just a small part of the problem.

2 'Panda Problems' is the best title as the extract lists a number of problems pandas face for survival. Natural enemies and bamboo dieback are only part of the problem.

3 Global warming is not listed as a threat to young pandas. It is not included in the extract.

4 Pandas are not aggressive animals. They are reluctant to protect their territory and move away when humans move in.

5 A timid animal is a shy animal. It may not be frightened.

6 The extract states that 'bamboos only flower every forty years'.

7 An animal becomes extinct when there are no living members of its species. If there are live animals of the species in a zoo, then it is not extinct.

Hearty Facts

1 written response 2 B 3 A 4 D 5 A 6 C 7 D

EXPLANATIONS

1 Possible answer:

Middle-aged people—that is, people over 40—are most likely to have a heart attack. Young people have a chance to care for their heart to prevent heart attacks later in life.

2 The best caption would be 'Eat healthy foods'. Sitting down or not working too hard would not fit the picture. Eating snacks between meals will not help your heart—unless they are healthy snacks!

3 The extract says that the heart needs help 'from its owner—you'. Each person is responsible for the health of their own heart—it's the individual's 'choice' to look after it.

4 Arteries are tubes in the body that carry blood. The word has nothing to do with 'art'.

5 If something is regular it has to happen often, or frequently. 'Weekly' is one example of something being regular, but is too specific. 'Reasonable' and 'gentle' are not quite correct.

6 The heart is one organ that never stops until we die. It is a big organ but not the largest. Its colour has nothing to do with being mighty. The word 'machine' suggests something that moves and operates like machinery, so 'C' is the best answer.

7 The best choice is that it is part of an explanation. The extract gives an 'explanation' on how to take care of your heart.

Tick each correct point.
Read the student's work through once to get an overall view of their response.

Focus on general points
- ☐ Did it make sense?
- ☐ Did it flow?
- ☐ Did the story arouse any feeling?
- ☐ Did you want to read on?
  Did the story create any suspense?
- ☐ Was the handwriting readable?

Now focus on the detail. Read each of the following points and find out whether the student's work has these features.

Focus on content
- ☐ Did the opening sentence(s) 'grab' the reader's interest?
- ☐ Was the setting established? (i.e. where the action takes place)
- ☐ Was the reader told when the action takes place?
- ☐ Was it clear who the main character(s) is/are? (The story can be in first person using *I*.)
- ☐ Was there a 'problem' to be solved early in the writing?
- ☐ Was a complication or unusual event introduced?
- ☐ Did descriptions refer to any of the senses? (e.g. *cold air, strange smell*)
- ☐ Was there a climax? (a more exciting part near the end)
- ☐ Was the conclusion (resolution of the problem) believable?

Focus on structure, vocabulary, grammar, spelling, punctuation
- ☐ Was there a variety of sentence lengths and beginnings?
- ☐ Was a new paragraph started for each change in time, place or action?
- ☐ Were conversations or direct speech in separate paragraphs for each change of speaker?
- ☐ Were adjectives used to improve descriptions? (e.g. <u>careful</u> steps)
- ☐ Were adverbs used to make actions more interesting? (e.g. *shook his head <u>sadly</u>*)
- ☐ Were capital letters used where they should have been?
- ☐ Was punctuation correct?

☐ Was the spelling of words correct?

Marker's suggestions (optional)

WRITING (Real Test)
Narrative text 2   Page 68

Tick each correct point.
Read the student's work through once to get an overall view of their response.

Focus on general points
- ☐ Did it make sense?
- ☐ Did it flow?
- ☐ Did the story arouse any feeling?
- ☐ Did you want to read on? Did the story create any suspense?
- ☐ Was the handwriting readable?

Now focus on the detail. Read each of the following points and find out whether the student's work has these features.

Focus on content
- ☐ Did the opening sentence(s) 'grab' the reader's interest?
- ☐ Was the setting established? (i.e. where the action takes place)
- ☐ Was the reader told when the action takes place?
- ☐ Was it apparent who the main character(s) is/are? (The story can be in first person using *I*.)
- ☐ Was there a 'problem' to be solved early in the writing?
- ☐ Was a complication or unusual event introduced?
- ☐ Did descriptions make reference to any of the senses? (e.g. *cold nose, warm coat*)
- ☐ Was there a climax? (a more exciting part near the end)
- ☐ Was the conclusion (resolution of the problem) believable?

Focus on structure, vocabulary, grammar, spelling, punctuation
- ☐ Was there a variation in sentence lengths and beginnings?

☐ Was a new paragraph started for each change in time, place or action?

☐ Were conversations or direct speech in separate paragraphs for each change of speaker?

☐ Were adjectives used to improve descriptions? (e.g. *hollow* sound)

☐ Were adverbs used to make actions more interesting? (e.g. *listened* *carefully*)

☐ Were capital letters where they should have been?

☐ Was punctuation correct?

☐ Was the spelling of words correct?

Marker's suggestions (optional)

WEEK 4

NUMBER AND ALGEBRA/STATISTICS AND PROBABILITY (Test Your Skills)
Patterns, algebra, chance and probability   Page 70

Patterns and algebra

1 $6 \times 4 = 24$ and $2 \times 12 = 24$.

2 Option A is doubling, Option C is adding one, and Option D is subtracting 2. Option B is the correct answer.

3 $18 \div 9 = 2$, therefore $9 \times 2 = 18$.

4 The pattern is increasing by an extra one for each new term: $3 + 1 = 4$, then $4 + 2 = 6$, then $6 + 3 = 9$. So $9 + 4 = 13$.

5 $6 + 5 = 11$, and $11 - 2 = 9$.

6 There are four 15s to be added. This is the same as four lots of 15, or 4×15. This can be written as 15×4.

7 The number in the bottom line is four more than the number in the top line, so $13 + 4 = 17$.

8 There are two less stars in each row. There will be no stars in the next row.

Chance and probability

1 There is 1 chance in 6 for any number to appear after one toss of a die.

2 There will most likely be cold days in winter. Winter is the coldest season.

3 Half $\left(\dfrac{1}{2}\right)$ the blocks are red and half $\left(\dfrac{1}{2}\right)$ the blocks are green. Tim therefore has 1 chance in 2 of selecting a red block.

4 Six three-digit numbers can be made with 6, 9 and 4:
they are 469, 496, 649, 694, 946 and 964.

5 Myra will most likely get a black when she spins her spinner. There are 2 chances out of 6, or 1 in 3. There is only a 1 in 6 chance that she will spin another colour.

6 More vans went past in the hour (17), so a van is most likely to be the next vehicle.

NUMBER AND ALGEBRA/STATISTICS AND PROBABILITY (Real Test)
Patterns, algebra, chance and probability   Page 73

1 B   2 D   3 5   4 C   5 A   6 C   7 B   8 C   9 C   10 D
11 A   12 C   13 A   14 D   15 5   16 C

EXPLANATIONS

1 11 24 37
The numbers are counting forward by 13.
Next number $= 37 + 13$
$= 37 + 3 + 10$
$= 40 + 10$
$= 50$

2 Consider the choices; here are some of them:
11 and 32 have a difference of 21
27 and 42 have a difference of 15
27 and 46 have a difference of 19
32 and 46 have a difference of 14

3 12 + 12 + 12 + 12 + 12 = 5 × 12

4 The numbers are counting backwards by 8, as 85 − 77 = 8.
Next number = 61 − 8
= 61 − 1 − 7
= 60 − 7
= 53

5 'what number' times 3 is 33. The number would be 11 as 11 × 3 = 33.

6 Melanie is counting forwards by 3:
    3, 6, 9, 12, 15, 18, 21, 24
The eighth number is 24.

7 The second row in the table has numbers that are counting forward by 4.
Missing number = 16 + 4
= 20.

8 25, 35, 45, 55, 65: count forward by 10
5, 50, 500, 5000, 50 000: multiply by 10
40, 45, 50, 55, 60: counting forward by 5
5, 55, 555, 5555, 55 555: placing a 5 on
        the end of each number
The correct answer is 40, 45, 50, 55, 60.

9 Consider the number at the front of each number sentence: 40, 50, 60, 90. To move from 60 to 90, we add 30.
Now check the end of each number sentence: 24, 34, 44, ____. This means we add 30 on to 44 to get 74.

10 Comparing the diagrams: 1, 3, 6, 10, __.
Starting at 1, then *added 2*, then *added 3*, then *added 4*, so we need to *add 5*. The next number will be 15.

11 Next number = 72 − 6
= 72 − 2 − 4
= 70 − 4
= 66

12 Three of the sections are yellow, which means it is the most likely colour.

13 There are 6 faces on the die and only one is a 4. The chance of rolling a 4 is one out of 6, or 1 in 6.

14 The chance of the sun rising is certain.

15 Total of black and red = 12 + 3
= 15
No. of green jelly beans = 20 − 15
= 5
There must be 5 green jelly beans.

16 There are 3 red jelly beans out of the total 20. This means the chance of a red jelly bean is 3 out of 20.

> **STATISTICS AND PROBABILITY**
> **(Test Your Skills)**
> *Graphs, tables and data*   Page 74

1 David and Lorenz both scored 23.

2 Melody must score 15 to score higher than Joyce, who scored 25. 11 + 15 = 26.

3 Jamie spent a quarter of his money on fast food and another quarter on a T-shirt. The sectors for these two items are the same size.

4 There are 13 phones in the factory (3 + 3 + 3 + 4 = 13).

5 The tally represents 17 (5 + 5 + 5 + 2 = 17).

6 Class 4H sold 16 family portraits.

7 Five classes took part in the project (2E, 3D, 4H, 5W, 6M).

8 Juice is the most preferred drink (8 boys + 7 girls = 15 altogether).

9 The total number of boys is 4 + 8 + 2 + 8 = 22.

> **STATISTICS AND PROBABILITY (Real Test)**
> *Graphs, tables and data*   Page 76

1 C **2** C **3** B **4** D **5** C **6** A **7** D **8** B **9** B **10** A
11 A **12** B **13** A **14** 3 **15** B **16** C

EXPLANATIONS

1 From the graph, there are 4 pie symbols for year 3. This means 4 × 10 = 40 pies.

2 Year 3 sold 40 pies, year 4 (30), year 5 (10) and year 6 (20). This means that 3 year groups sold more than 15 pies.

3 Total pie symbols = 4 + 3 + 1 + 2
                              = 10
As 10 × 10 = 100, the school has sold 100 pies in total. This means profit is found by multiplying 100 by 2.
Profit = 100 × 2
          = 200.
The profit is $200

4 12 students chose netball, while 9 chose swimming, 9 chose basketball and 6 chose soccer. This means that netball is the favourite sport.

5 Basketball makes up 9 or one quarter of the students.
 No. who chose basketball = 36 ÷ 4
                                       = 9
This means about 9 people chose basketball.

6 The graph shows 6 students walked to school.

7 From the graph we can see bike (8 students), bus (12), walk (6) and car (4).
Total = 8 + 12 + 6 + 4
        = 30
This means that 30 students were surveyed.

8 From the graph, 12 students caught the bus in the morning. In the afternoon 2 students did not catch the bus.
Number who caught bus = 12 – 2
                                     = 10
There were 10 students who caught the bus in the afternoon.

9 The second row of the table shows the number of each age group at the holiday club.
Total = 4 + 6 + 12 + 8 + 4 + 5
        = 10 + 20 + 9
        = 39
This means there were 39 children at the holiday club.

10 More than 10 years old means 11 year old: 4 and 12 years old: 5
Total over 10s = 4 + 5
                     = 9
This means that there are 9 children over the age of 10 years old.

11 Add the laps 8 + 6 + 12 + 10 = 36.
If Quentin swam a total of 40 laps, we can find the number on Thursday by subtraction.
Thursday laps = 40 – 36
                     = 4
Quentin swam 4 laps on Thursday

12 On Wednesday and Friday he swam more than 8 laps.
This means he swam more than 8 laps on 2 days.

13 Compare each of the amounts: the highest amount is $2.90. Bree spent the most money.

14 Consider each answer, and there are 3 people who spent at least $2.

15 $2.90 is closer to $3 than $2
$0.80 is closer to $1 than $0
$2.25 is closer to $2 than $3
$2.05 is closer to $2 than $3
Total = 3 + 1 + 2 + 2
        = 8
The best estimate is $8.

16 The number of males is found by adding the numbers in the row titled 'males'.
Number of males = 4 + 11
                        = 15
This means that there were 15 males at the party.

SPELLING (Real Test)
Common misspellings   Page 78

1 **a** once **b** balloon **c** using **d** uncle **e** fried
f ready **g** cheered **h** any

2 **a** water **b** cover **c** spout **d** kettle

3 **a** down **b** running **c** someone **d** window **e** followed **f** knock

GRAMMAR AND PUNCTUATION (Real Test)
Adverbs, prepositions, pronouns and apostrophes   **Pages 80–81**

1 A 2 C 3 C 4 D 5 B 6 A 7 D 8 A 9 C 10 B
11 C 12 D 13 B 14 D 15 C 16 D 17 A 18 B

1 *Use* is when talking about one person or thing.

2 *Hour* begins with a silent *h*. The train took an hour.

3 *It's* is the short form of *it is*.

4 The speed of the truck is described with an adverb. *Quickly* is correct.

5 *Broke* is the correct verb. 'Breaked' is not a word and not the past tense of *break*.

6 The correct preposition in this situation is *around*.

7 Three commas are required. No comma is needed before *and*. *On our holiday we saw lighthouses, museums, markets, bridges and towers.*

8 The correct preposition in this situation is *in*: *Today, in the paper ...*

9 When referring to people, use the personal pronoun *who*.

10 The way the door opened is described by an adverb. *Slowly* is correct.

11 *Alien* begins with a vowel. *An* is correct: *an alien*.

12 *Its* is correct. A capital letter is required as it is the start of a new sentence. *Its* is a possessive pronoun and does not need an apostrophe.

13 *Or* is correct: *It had no ... nose or even a mouth.* No comma is required between *nose* and *or*.

14 The word *somebody* is a compound word. It is a pronoun and does not take a capital.

15 This sentence is best as an exclamation sentence. *Can't* is short for *cannot*. *Won't* is short for *will not*.

16 *Better* is correct. It is used to show the difference between two different times (before and after getting glasses).

17 The comma is used to separate items in a list. *And* separates the last two items. *For days, weeks and months we put up with drought and dust.*

18 This is a question. The correct possessive pronoun is *my*.

READING (Test Your Skills)
Following procedures   **Page 82**

Chocolate Milk Drift

1 There are eight steps to get the drink ready for serving, including adding the straw. Each step is numbered.

2 Some people may leave out the sugar—it is only added for individual or personal taste 'if required'.

3 The word 'instant' in the recipe means 'ready for use'. 'Prepared' suggests something that is ready to eat, or something that has been mixed up or started earlier, which is not the same as being ready to use. The other meanings of 'instant' relate to other uses of the word that do not apply to the recipe.

4 The steps of a recipe refer to the 'method' used to make the drink. 'Stage' usually refers to a longer period of time (e.g. 'this stage of the game'). 'Stairs' and 'levels' refer to height (as in staircases).

5 The next instruction (Step 4) is to put the bowl into fridge and chill.

6 The mixture makes 'four tall glasses' of Chocolate Milk Drift. It would serve four people. It also uses four scoops of icecream—one for each glass/person.

7 The bowl is used to mix and chill the mixture. The coffee mug is used to dissolve the instant chocolate powder. The glass is used to serve the drink. A saucepan is not required.

READING (Real Test)
Following procedures   Page 83

The Disappearing Assistant

1 A 2 B 3 A 4 C 5 A 6 D

EXPLANATIONS

1 This performance is a (magic) trick. It is not actual magic so would not be taught in a lesson on real magic! It's not for a TV show or a craft lesson.

2 An assistant is a person who helps (a helper). Even though the magic trick is performed before an audience, the assistant is not an actor.

3 The bottom of the box is made into a flap so that it can be lifted up and the assistant can stand on the floor. This allows the assistant to escape through the bottom.

4 This information is not in the text—you have to 'read between the lines'. If the audience is too close they will able to see the assistant hiding behind the box. The distance does not allow the assistant to escape, the size of the audience is not a factor, and the magician shouldn't make mistakes.

5 The assistant is a part of the trick. He or she has to know what to do, so the trick is well-planned (not unplanned). The magic words are part of tricking the audience. The trick would not be interesting if the audience knew how the assistant 'disappeared'.

6 The word 'adapted' means modified or changed slightly. This will be done to suit the purposes of the magician. The box is not destroyed or given away (be careful not to confuse 'adapted' with 'adopted'). It can be used for the trick a number of times, not just once.

READING (Test Your Skills)
Interpreting other texts   Page 84

Book Blurb

1 There are eight books in the set. The eight pictures of book covers which include Bubble Buster will give you this information.

2 The titles and the cover illustrations suggest that these books are meant to be amusing, not informative or factual. They look like they contain stories.

3 The cover and the title suggest that Look Out! Look Out! Tractor About! is a book set on a farm. Tractors are common on farms.

4 The cover of Zac's Story suggests that it is a book involving cricket.

5 If a book is said to be 'hard to put down' it means that the reader will want to keep reading it to the end. This suggests that readers will find the story fun, entertaining and/or very interesting.

6 The question 'Will Buster get home?', is meant to put a question in the reader's mind so the reader is encouraged to take up the book and find the answer. The person who wrote the blurb will know the answer to the question. It is not supposed to frighten readers, but aims to capture their interest.

7 Sparklers are 'safe' fireworks, often meant for younger children.

Check Your Answers

ANSWERS
Week 4

READING (Real Test)
Interpreting other texts Page 85

The Wind and the Sun

1 C 2 D 3 C 4 B 5 written response 6 A 7 A
EXPLANATIONS

1 The wind felt confident (sure) he would win. He had no doubts and wasn't worried.

2 For these questions you have to recognise the type of text you have been given. A fable is a story that has a lesson for the reader. It is not a report, which is usually factual. A legend tells an heroic story of great deeds from the past. The Wind and the Sun is not a fairy tale.

3 The wind tried to remove the traveller's coat by force, but the sun used gentle persuasion to encourage the traveller to take the coat off himself. 'All is fair in love and war' usually refers to a contest that is unfair. 'Truth is stranger than fiction' is not relevant because the story is not actually true. 'Many hands make light work' usually refers to a story of cooperation or people helping one another—the wind and the sun do not work together in this story.

4 The best answer is 'withstood', meaning 'resisted'. The traveller could not 'avoid' or 'ignore' the wind, and he did not 'help' the wind when the wind tried to remove the coat.

5 Possible answer:

The unknown traveller was just passing by as the sun and wind were deciding on their contest; he didn't have any choice.

6 A 'dispute' is a 'disagreement' or a small argument. It is used as a noun in the story, so it cannot be replaced by 'displease' or 'compete', which are verbs. 'Row' is too strong a word, as it indicates a very heated argument.

7 The sun and wind agreed to have a friendly contest, so they are 'competitors', not 'enemies' or 'fighters'. They didn't do anything wrong so they are not 'criminals'.

READING (Real Test)
Interpreting other texts Page 86

Dragon Boat Festival

1 D 2 C 3 A 4 C 5 B 6 A
EXPLANATIONS

1 The text tells the reader that Qu Yuan threw himself into the river because he was protesting against the government's actions. The fishermen and the boat races came later. The spirit referred to in the extract is the poet's spirit.

2 The food was not for the fish or the fishermen but to help Qu Yuan's spirit on its journey to heaven.

3 Qu Yuan drowned—that is why his spirit needed help on its journey. The dragon boat races started after his death. The fishermen scared the fish away from his body.

4 Dragon boat races are held yearly, usually in June (the fifth day of the fifth month in the Chinese lunar calendar).

5 The boats are built like dragons 'to please the spirit of the waters'.

6 'Traditionally' in this extract has a meaning closest to 'usually'. Try replacing 'traditionally' with the other words. 'Always' is a little too strong.

WRITING (Real Test)
Description of a place or scene Page 88

Tick each correct point.
Read the student's work through once to get an overall view of their response.
Focus on general points
☐ Did it make sense?
☐ Did it flow?

Excel Revise in a Month Year 3 NAPLAN*-style Tests **153**

☐ Did the description arouse the reader's interest?

☐ Did you want to read on to understand more about the place or scene?

☐ Was the handwriting readable?

Now focus on the detail. Read each of the following points and find out whether the student's work has these features.

Focus on content

☐ Is the general scene and basic location clearly stated?

☐ Has the writer provided some physical description of the scene or landscape?

☐ Is the description broken up into parts (e.g. sea, sand, cliffs)?

☐ Has the writer tried to put the scene in a time frame (e.g. a late autumn day)?

(optional)

☐ Is relevant detail included? (e.g. *soft, golden sand*)

☐ Does the language create clear pictures?

☐ Does the writer make reference to reactions to the scene through several senses? (e.g. *cool water*)

☐ Does the writer convey any feelings created by the scene?

☐ Is there a concluding comment, opinion or reaction to the scene?

Focus on structure, vocabulary, grammar, spelling, punctuation

☐ Is the description written in present tense?

☐ Is there variation in sentence lengths and beginnings?

☐ Are there paragraphs separating different aspects of the scene?

☐ Has the writer used any similes? (e.g. *as clear as glass*)

☐ Is there a generous use of adjectives to enhance the writing? (e.g. _cool_, _shady_ grass)

☐ Are adverbs used effectively? (e.g. *lying lazily on the sand*)

☐ Are capital letters used correctly?

☐ Is the punctuation correct?

☐ Is the spelling of words correct?

Practical suggestion: ask yourself if you can visualise the scene.

Marker's suggestions (optional)

WRITING (Real Test)
Description of a person Page 89

Tick each correct point.
Read the student's work through once to get an overall view of their response.

Focus on general points

☐ Did it make sense?

☐ Did it flow?

☐ Did the description arouse the reader's interest?

☐ Did you want to read on to understand more about the person or animal?

☐ Was the handwriting readable?

Now focus on the detail. Read each of the following points and find out whether the student's work has these features.

Focus on content

☐ Has the character to be described been established?

☐ Has the writer provided some physical description of the person?

☐ Is the description broken up into parts? (e.g. appearance, mannerisms, age, interests)

☐ Is relevant detail included? (e.g. hair colour)

☐ Does the language create clear pictures?

☐ Does the writer make reference to reactions to the person through several senses? (e.g. *wiry hair, soft skin*)

☐ Does the writer convey any feelings about the character?

☐ Is there a concluding comment, opinion or reaction to the character (can be reflective)?

Focus on structure, vocabulary, grammar, spelling, punctuation

☐ Is the description written in present tense?

☐ Is there variation in sentence lengths and beginnings?

☐ Are there paragraphs separating different aspects of the character?

☐ Has the writer used any similes? (e.g. *as thin as a rake*)

- ☐ Is there a generous use of adjectives to enhance the writing? (e.g. *long, bony fingers*)
- ☐ Are adverbs used effectively? (e.g. *smiled happily*)
- ☐ Are capital letters used correctly?
- ☐ Is the punctuation correct?
- ☐ Is the spelling of words correct?

Practical suggestion: ask yourself if you can visualise the person described.

Marker's suggestions (optional)

WRITING (Real Test)
Explanation Page 90

Tick each correct point.
Read the student's work through once to get an overall view of their response.

Focus on general points
- ☐ Did it make sense?
- ☐ Did it flow?
- ☐ Did the writing and subject arouse the reader's interest?
- ☐ Did you want to read on?
- ☐ Was the handwriting readable?

Now focus on the detail. Read each of the following points and find out whether the student's work has these features.

Focus on content
- ☐ Do the introductory sentences clearly identify (and define) the subject?
- ☐ Are the features of the subject precisely described? (colour, size, shape, etc.)
- ☐ Does the information sound factual?
- ☐ Are the uses of the subject explained?
- ☐ Is there any information explaining specific or unusual instances of use? (optional)
- ☐ Does the writer suggest who would use the item selected?
- ☐ Does the writer give a concluding comment, opinion or personal judgment of the subject?

Focus on structure, vocabulary, grammar, spelling, punctuation
- ☐ Is there variation in sentence lengths and beginnings?
- ☐ Have 'longer' sentences been used? (including multiple clauses beginning with words such as *so, because, when* and *if*)
- ☐ Are the sections broken up into clear paragraphs?
- ☐ Are the paragraphs based on single topics? (e.g. shape, colour, how to use, etc.)
- ☐ Have subheadings been used? (optional)
- ☐ Have technical or scientific (correct) words been used?
- ☐ Is the explanation written in the present tense?
- ☐ Are adjectives used to enhance the writing? (e.g. *colourful pattern*)
- ☐ Are capital letters used correctly?
- ☐ Is the punctuation correct?
- ☐ Is the spelling of words correct?

Practical suggestion: ask yourself if this explanation provides enough information for you to use the object or draw a picture of it.

Marker's suggestions (optional)

SAMPLE TEST PAPERS

SAMPLE TEST PAPER 1

LITERACY – WRITING Page 92

Persuasive text

Tick each correct point.
Read the student's work through once to get an overall view of their response.

Focus on general points
- ☐ Did it make sense?
- ☐ Did it flow? Were the arguments logical and relevant?

☐ Did the opinions expressed arouse any feelings/reactions?

☐ Was the body of the writing mainly in the third person?

☐ Did you want to read on to understand/ appreciate the writer's point of view?

☐ Were the arguments convincing?

☐ Has the writer been assertive (e.g. the use of *is* rather than a less definite term)?

☐ Was the handwriting readable?

☐ Was the writing style suitable for a persuasive text (objective; not casual or dismissive)?

Now focus on the detail. Read each of the following points and find out whether the student's work has these features.

Focus on content

☐ Did the opening sentence(s) focus on the topic?

☐ Was the writer's point of view established early in the writing?

☐ Did the writer include any evidence to support his or her opinion?

☐ Did the writer include information relevant to his or her experiences?

☐ Were the points/arguments raised by the writer easy to follow?

☐ Did the writing follow the format with an introduction, the body of the text and a conclusion?

☐ Were personal opinions included?

☐ Was the concluding paragraph relevant to the topic?

Focus on structure, vocabulary, grammar, spelling, punctuation

☐ Was there a variety of sentence lengths, types and beginnings?

☐ Was a new paragraph started for each additional argument or point?

☐ Has the writer used any similes (e.g. *as clear as crystal*) to stress a point raised?

☐ Did the writer avoid approximations such as *probably, perhaps* and *maybe*?

☐ Did the writer use such phrases as *I know …* and *It is important to …*?

☐ Did the writer refer to the question in the points raised (A good way to do this is to use the key words from the question or the introduction.)?

☐ Has the writer used any less common words correctly?

☐ Was indirect speech used correctly?

☐ Were adjectives used to improve descriptions (e.g. <u>expensive</u> *buildings*)?

☐ Were adverbs used effectively (e.g. *firstly*)?

☐ Were capital letters used correctly?

☐ Was punctuation used correctly?

☐ Was the spelling of words correct?

Marker's suggestions (optional)

LITERACY – LANGUAGE CONVENTIONS
Pages 93–96

1 board **2** germs **3** least **4** pilot **5** shock
6 ours **7** zebra **8** hopeless **9** ponies **10** view
11 plane **12** cabin **13** swept **14** tail **15** tools
16 biting **17** tasks **18** apple **19** table
20 entries **21** believed **22** something
23 plate **24** carrot **25** through **26** C **27** C
28 A **29** B **30** C **31** B **32** A **33** D **34** B **35** A
36 C **37** B **38** D **39** A **40** D **41** C **42** B **43** B
44 C **45** A **46** C **47** D **48** B **49** C **50** A

EXPLANATIONS

1 The correct spelling is *board*, not *bored*.
Tip: *Bored* and *board* sound the same. Learn the different spellings of words that sound the same, in this case *board* (timber) and *bored* (not interested). Learn when to use them correctly.

2 The correct spelling is *germs*, not 'jerms'.
Tip: Many words that begin with a *g* often sound as if they begin with a *j*. Become familiar which common words that have this feature (e.g. *gentle, gem*).

3 The correct spelling is *least*, not 'laest'.
Tip: The letters *e* and *a* have swapped positions. Take care not to reverse letter

order. Learn to recognise word groups with similar spellings (e.g. *beast*, *feast*).

4 The correct spelling is *pilot*, not 'pilote'.
Tip: It is easy to add an e to words that end in commonly used consonants. Say the last syllable silently to see if it sounds correct.

5 The correct spelling is *shock*, not 'schock'.
Tip: Although c can often follows s, it does not in *shock*.

6 The correct spelling is *ours*, not 'ourse'.
Tip: Make sure you pronounce the word correctly. There are quite a few words that end with 'urse' (*purse*, *curse*) but this is not one of them. *Ours* is a common word and it is important that you can spell it correctly.

7 The correct spelling is *zebra*, not 'zebera'.
Tip: Make sure you pronounce the word correctly. *Zebra* has two syllables, not three.

8 The correct spelling is *hopeless*, not 'hopless'.
Tip: Think of the word without the *less* ending. There is quite a difference between *hop* and *hope*.

9 The correct spelling is *ponies*, not 'ponys'.
Tip: When making a plural with a word that ends with consonant + *y*, change the *y* to *i* and add *es* (e.g. *berry—berries*, *spy—spies*).

10 The correct spelling is *view*, not 'veiw'.
Tip: In many *ie* words the *i* comes before the *e* (e.g. *field*, *piece*) although there are quite a few exceptions. It is important to be familiar with the correct spelling of similar common words.

11 The correct spelling is *plane*, not *plain*.
Tip: Learn the different spellings of words that sound the same, in this case *plain* (ordinary) and *plane* (aircraft). Learn when to use them correctly.

12 The correct spelling is *cabin*, not 'caben'.
Tip: Make sure you pronounce the word carefully and correctly. Remember: *robin* has a similar spelling.

13 The correct spelling is *swept*, not 'sweept'.
Tip: Make sure you pronounce the word carefully and correctly. The past tense of *sweep* is *swept*. Learn to recognise word groups with similar spellings (e.g. *kept*, *crept*).

14 The correct spelling is *tail*, not *tale*.
Tip: Learn the different spellings of words that sound the same, in this case *tail* (end part) and *tale* (story). Learn when to use them correctly.

15 The correct spelling is *tools*, not 'tules'.
Tip: 'Tules' is not a word. Learn to recognise word groups with similar spellings (e.g. *fools*, *pools*). The 'ule' and 'ool' word endings sound the same (rhyme) but they often have different spellings (*rule*, *cool*).

16 The misspelled word is *biting*.
Tip: Words that end with a consonant + *e* drop the *e* before adding a suffix beginning with a vowel (*write—writing*).

17 The misspelled word is *tasks*.
Tip: Make sure you pronounce the word carefully and correctly. Remember: *asks* and *flasks* have similar spellings.

18 The misspelled word is *apple*.
Tip: Apple has a double *p* (*pp*) but not a double *l* (*ll*).

19 The misspelled word is *table*.
Tip: The *le* ending is more common (*ankle*, *able*).

20 The misspelled word is *entries*.
Tip: When making a plural with a word that ends with consonant + *y*, change the *y* to i and add *es* (e.g. *lady—ladies*, *bully—bullies*).

21 The misspelled word is *believed*.
Tip: In *believe* the *ie* has an *ee* sound. Learn to recognise and spell word groups with similar spellings (*relieve*, *grieve*).

22 The misspelled word is *something*.
Tip: Make sure you pronounce the word carefully and correctly. The word is *something*, not 'somethink'.

23 The misspelled word is *plate*.
Tip: The letters *ate* and *ait* can sound the same. You should recognise and remember when to use the different spelling (e.g. *bait*, *rate*). Get to know groups of words with similar spellings.

24 The misspelled word is *carrot*.
Tip: Carrot has a double *r* (*rr*). Learn to recognise word groups with similar spellings (e.g. *parrot*).

25 The misspelled word is *through*.
Tip: Learn the different spellings of words that sound the same, in this case *through* (to move from one place to another) and *threw* (past tense of the word *throw*). Learn when to use them correctly.

26 *Ahead* is unnecessary. It is a redundant word. It carries the same meaning as *plan*. Plans can only be made *ahead* of an event, such as a holiday. Plans are always for the future.

27 This is a grammar and spelling question. The correct word is *who*.
Tip: *Who* is used when referring to people.

28 This is a grammar question. The adjectives are *fast*, *merry*, *lazy* and *faithful*.
Tip: Adjectives are describing words most often used before nouns.

29 This is a grammar question. The correct word is *feet*.
Tip: There is more than one foot so the correct plural is *feet*. 'Foots' and 'feets' are not real words.

30 This is a grammar question. The correct word is the preposition *towards*.
Tip: Prepositions put events in position in time or place. We use *towards* to show the direction in which Jay is plodding.

31 This is a punctuation question. The correct sentence is: *"It's not ours but do you want to use it?"* asked Brendan.
Tip: Question marks (?) go at the end of questions. This question mark goes at the end of the question Brendan asked, but it must go inside the quotation marks (" and ").

32 This is a grammar question. The correct word is *didn't*.
Tip: This question has two parts: You did do your corrections, / didn't you? Questions like this one begin with a statement and finish with a mini-question (tag), often using the word not in the mini-question.

33 This is a grammar question. The correct word is *of*.
Tip: Prepositions put events in position in time or place. Use *of* to separate two nouns (*days* and *white settlement*).

34 This is a grammar question. The correct word is *or*.
Tip: *Or* is used because you are given an option—either trains or trucks.

35 This is a grammar question. The correct word is *were*.
Tip: Basic rule: Singular subjects (nouns) need singular verbs; plural subjects (nouns) need plural verbs. In this sentence, *were* must be used because there are many loads. The word *was* is used when there is just one load: *A heavy load* <u>was</u> ...

36 This is a punctuation question. The correct punctuation is *teams.* (with the full stop).
Tip: *Teams* is the last word in the sentence and should be followed by a full stop. The next sentence starts with *Every*.

37 This is a grammar question. The correct word is *the*.
Tip: *The* refers to a particular type of camp —logging camps. It is not any type of camp, which would be implied by *a camp*.

38 This is a grammar question. The correct word is *brought*.
Tip: *Brought* is an irregular verb. Most verbs in English form their past tenses by adding *ed*. There are a number of irregular verbs where this doesn't happen. We say *brought* instead of 'bringed'. 'Brang' is not a real word. *Bought* comes from *buy*.

39 This is a punctuation question. The correct sentence is: *Jim's shoes were dropped in the park and now James can't find them.*
Tip: The apostrophe shows that Jim owns the shoes. James doesn't own anything.

40 This is a punctuation question. The correct sentence is: *Whatever the season, weekends in December are my favourite time.*
Tip: The only proper noun in this sentence is *December*. *Seasons* and *Weekends* are common nouns and don't take a capital letter.

41 This is a grammar question. The correct word is *bit*.
Tip: *Bit* is an irregular verb. Most verbs in English form their past tenses by adding *ed*. There are a number of irregular verbs when this doesn't happen. We say *bit* instead of 'bited'. *Bitten* is part of a verb and needs a helper such as *was* (*was bitten*).

42 This is a grammar question. The correct word is *however*.
Tip: *However* is a conjunction and is used to indicate that even though Leanne had hurt her wrist, she was still able to make pancakes.

43 This is a punctuation question. The correct sentence is: *Jill and I don't have hiking boots(.) We have backpacks and all our other clothes.*
Tip: Full stops go at the end of statements. There are two statements: *We have backpacks and all our other clothes.* has its full stop. The beginning of the sentence is

We. The full stop goes after *boots*. Look for places where there will be pauses in the sentence.

44 This is a punctuation question. The correct sentence is: *The tree, which was struck by lightning, will have to be removed.*
Tip: The comma (,) suggests that there should be a pause and is used to show separate parts of a statement: *The tree, which was struck by lightning, will …* The words *which was struck by lightning* indicate which tree is being referred to.

45 This is a grammar question. The unnecessary word is *two*.
Tip: *Two* is unnecessary. It is superfluous. Twins are always in pairs (twos). No meaning is lost by omitting *two*.

46 This is a grammar question. The correct sentence is: *The day was cold and there were few people on the beach.*
Tip: *Much* and *few* are used to show an amount of something. *Few* is used with things that can be counted—*few people*. *Much* and *little* are used with things that are not counted—*much sand/little sand*.

47 This is a punctuation question. The correct sentence is: *As Tyron climbed up the ladder he shouted to his mother, "How much higher?"*
Tip: Speech marks (" and ") open and close the words that are spoken. The speech marks (quotation marks) open with the word *How* and close after the question mark that follows the word *higher*.

48 This is a grammar question. The correct word is *cool*.
Tip: For questions like this one you have to know the precise meaning of the word. The sun had gone down after a warm day. The verb *cool* suggests that the temperature was dropping. *Cold* is an adjective when referring to weather conditions.

49 This is a grammar question. The correct word is *faster*.
Tip: The word *faster* is used when comparing the speed of two things. Firstly it is the speed of Jill and Cara. Then it is the speed of Cara and the whole of another team. *Fastest* is used when comparing more than two speeds. *More faster* is incorrect usage.

50 This is a grammar question. The correct answer is *have done*.
Tip: *Done* is past tense. This has already happened. *I have done every sum* lets the reader know that you have finished your sums. With the verb *done* you need the correct 'helper'—another verb to 'help' it. *Have*, *has* and *had* can be helping verbs: *I have done*. The word *done* by itself is incorrect. *Has done* would be used when speaking about someone else (e.g. *Jack has done*).

LITERACY – READING   Pages 97–103

Drawing Stars

1 B 2 A 3 C 4 B 5 D 6 C

EXPLANATIONS

1 Five separate lines are required to draw a five-pointed star following the instructions.

2 Rub out the inside lines before you colour it in.

3 You need to practise drawing on scrap paper. It may take several goes before you get a neat looking star.

4 The arrowheads show the direction to draw each line. The arrow heads are not part of the star. They are not meant to show speed.

5 When you feel confident drawing stars beginning at the top, try drawing stars starting at different points. Six-pointed stars have simpler directions to follow.

6 You have to know the terms used to describe different types of writing. The author has written this information to provide instructions on how to draw stars.

Dingo

7 D 8 A 9 C 10 B 11 D 12 A

EXPLANATIONS

7 A canine is a type of dog. A dingo is a type of wild dog and a canine mammal.

8 Dingos are most often (usually) ginger. Sometimes they are black.

9 Erect means in an upright position – standing up. It has sharp ears, not floppy ears.

10 The name given to the ends (tips) of the snout, ears and feet is points.

11 A pack animal is an animal that hunts other animals as a group, or in packs. It has nothing to do with living as a group.

12 Female dingos have litters of different numbers. They give birth to between one and eight pups three or four times a year. A litter is the name for a group of young animals born at the same time to the same mother.

A Pirate's Life

13 C 14 B 15 A 16 D 17 A

EXPLANATIONS

13 A wanted man is a man wanted by the police.

14 Plunder is goods stolen (often from a ship). Booty is another word for goods stolen.

15 Life was harsh. A man might be hanged for stealing food to feed his family.

16 Pirates were better paid than sailors because pirates got a share of the stolen goods.

17 Booty is goods stolen from ships at sea.

Houseboats

18 C   **19** B   **20** D   **21** A   **22** B

EXPLANATIONS

18 Houseboats would be unstable in rough seas or on ocean voyages because they have flat bottoms. Items on deck could be washed overboard.

19 *Moored* is the word used to say a boat is tied up or anchored in a fixed position.

20 Owners of houseboats would not be able to grow a garden. They are surrounded by water. Owners can use mobile phones because they are moored near land. As they don't go on long sea voyages they would rarely be out of range. In wet weather, the boat would be similar to a house.

21 Houseboats would be suitable for a retired person. Elderly couples and families with children might find houseboat living unsafe or difficult for school and work. Babies could easily fall from the deck.

22 A junk can be used as a passenger boat. If a junk is used as a houseboat it would have sleeping accommodation. As a cargo boat, a junk could be used outside China.

Dog on a Diet

23 C   **24** written response   **25** D   **26** A   **27** B   **28** C

EXPLANATIONS

23 Dog on a Diet would be an amusing book. The title and cover picture suggest this. The blurb on the back covers suggests that the dog is mischievous and gets into trouble.

24 Joan Dalgleish was an actor on stage, TV and radio before becoming an author.

25 Simon James owns Strider. Joan Dalgleish wrote the story. Stephen Axelsen was the illustrator. Strider is the dog's name.

26 It is a look of satisfaction on Strider's face. The text also suggests that Strider is quite happy to do something about his situation.

27 Strider is put on a diet because prices are going up and Mr James cannot afford to buy a lot of food to feed him.

28 The unanswered question is meant to encourage people to buy the book to find out what happens.

Ben

29 D   **30** C   **31** A   **32** B   **33** C   **34** D

EXPLANATIONS

29 Ben was not ready for changes in his life.

30 At Show and Tell Ben would not speak. Ben would shake his head and smile.

31 Ben was timid. This means he was shy and quiet. He did not get too involved. Feeble simply means weak.

32 The teachers were considerate. They tried to get Ben to join in. They didn't get annoyed, impatient or upset.

33 Ben took a photograph for Show and Tell. He sometimes took a toy.

34 Ben could do sums correctly. He could also read and write. He didn't speak in class so he couldn't give class reports.

Teeth

35 B   **36** written response   **37** D   **38** C   **39** A   **40** B

EXPLANATIONS

35 Ten teeth. You have to find the upper gum and count the (deciduous) teeth.

36 Twelve years of age. This is the lowest diagram in 'How teeth change'.

37 Incisors are the largest teeth actually showing through the gum of a one-year-old's mouth. You have to look at the diagram carefully.

38 Babies don't have bicuspids. You have to compare the labels on the upper and lower deciduous and permanent teeth diagrams.

39 The molar is the last tooth to come through. At age twelve it is still below the skin in the gum.

40 Four deciduous teeth are left. Remember the diagram only shows one side of the mouth. There are two similar teeth on the other side.

NUMERACY Pages 104–109

1 D 2 C 3 2.85 4 6 5 C 6 C 7 D 8 B 9 A
10 15.95 11 D 12 B 13 C 14 A 15 C 16 4 17 A
18 90 19 D 20 C 21 A 22 A 23 A 24 5 25 D
26 B 27 C 28 10 29 C 30 97 31 B 32 145 33 58
34 A 35 A

EXPLANATIONS

1 Consider $37 = 3 \times 10 + 7 \times 1$. This means 3 groups of 10 and 7 separate squares.

2 To find the number of packets, we use division:
No. of packets = $12 \div 4$
= 3
She can buy 3 packets of toilet rolls
No. of toilet rolls = 3×8
= 24
Yvonne can buy 24 toilet rolls for $12.

3 Cost = $1.60 + $1.25
= $2.85
It will cost $2.85 for the sandwich and milk.

$$\begin{array}{r} 1.60 \\ + 1.25 \\ \hline 2.85 \end{array}$$

4 From the table, Maddie read 6 pages on Wednesday. The answer is 6 pages.

5 The shape has 2 triangles out of the four shaded. This means half is shaded.

6 Theo has 18 coins because 6 times 3 is 18. When he places them in rows of 5, he will use 15 coins and have 3 left over.

7 The tallest building is D.

8 Conrad needs to travel north along Lee Street and then east along George Street.

9 The largest angle is the one that opens the greatest distance.

10 Price of chain = $12.55 + $3.40
= $15.95
The price of the chain is $15.95.

$$\begin{array}{r} 12.55 \\ + 3.40 \\ \hline 15.95 \end{array}$$

11 From the graph, Year 3: $40, Year 4: $35, Year 5: $20, Year 6: $30.
As $20 is half of $40, Year 5 raised half as much as Year 3.

12 We are looking for 2 numbers that add to 28 and have a difference of 4.
The 2 numbers are 16 and 12. This means Li receives 16 stickers and Shane receives 12 stickers.
Shane receives 12 stickers.

13 C, E and H are identical when flipped over the dotted line. When S is flipped the image is not the same as the original S.

14 As a hexagon has 6 sides and a pentagon has 5 sides, the total so far is $6 + 5 = 11$.
Number of sides in 3rd shape = $14 - 11$
= 3
The third shape has 3 sides and is a triangle.

15 Consider each of the choices:
78 is 8 away from 70
81 is 11 away from 70
68 is 2 away from 70
74 is 4 away from 70
As 68 is the closest to 70, Matheus's result is closest to 70.

16 If she sells 6 plants for $18, it means that each plant sells for $3. For Miriam to make $12, she needs to sell 4 plants because $12 divided by 4 gives $3.

17 To find the number of students left over, we divide 25 by 3 and find the remainder:
$25 \div 3 = 8$ and remainder 1.
This means that there will be one student left over.

18 Counting forward by 19 means we add 71 and 19:
Next number $= 71 + 19$
$= 71 + 20 - 1$
$= 91 - 1$
$= 90$
The next number is 90

19 When we add the three biggest numbers we have $4 + 5 + 2$, which is 11. It is impossible to get a total of 12.

20 The necklace repeats the pattern:
R B B G Y Y
This means for every green (G) she uses 2 yellow (Y) beads. As Lexie counts 6 green beads, she must have 12 yellow beads.

21 From the table, the numbers that are larger than 50 are 68, 52 and 63. This means that there are 3 students who have more than 50 stored phone numbers.

22 The grid can contain a total of 14 rectangles. As there are already 3 rectangles, Karl will need another 11 rectangles.

23 The soup is on the middle shelf, second from the left.

24 Work backwards from John's answer of 6. Adding 4 gives 10. Half of 10 is 5. This means that John's number is 5.

25 There are 7 triangles in the shape:

26 On the spinner are the numbers:
1: 2 times, 2: 3 times; 3: 3 times.
'It is more likely to spin an even number than an odd number' is NOT true as there are only 3 even numbers and 5 odd numbers.

27 There are 4 symbols for Katie's Not Alone. As each symbol represents 3 students,
No. of students $= 4 \times 3$
$= 12$
This means 12 students watched Katie's Not Alone.

28 She started with 10 because when she doubled it she got 20 and then taking away 3 gives 17. If she wanted to do it all in reverse, she would start with 17 then add 3 to get 20 and then halve to make 10.

29 To find the total number of balls we multiply the number of buckets by the number of balls in each bucket: 6×3

30 The numbers have a last digit 7 and the pattern of the other digits is 15, 13, 11, ___. The next number would be a 9. This means that the missing number is 97.
We could have found this number by subtraction:
New number $= 117 - 20$
$= 117 - 17 - 3$
$= 100 - 3$
$= 97$

31 First, find the games where Blues score more than Reds:
Game 1 $32 - 20 = 12$
Game 2 $44 - 38 = 4$
Game 3   Reds win
Game 4 $38 - 22 = 16$
There were 2 games when Blues defeated Reds by more than 10 points.

32 The number line is going up by 5s. The middle number is 145.

33 Each day the 3 children take 2 tablets each. This means that 6 tablets are taken each day. As there are 7 days in a week, then 7 times 6 is 42. Finally, subtracting 42 from 100 gives 58. After a week there are 58 tablets left in the bottle.

34 The original shape is:

When it is turned a quarter turn the image is:

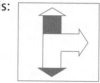

35 The only cube without paint is the one in the middle of the large cube. This means that there is 1 cube.

SAMPLE TEST PAPER 2

LITERACY – WRITING   Page 110

Description

Tick each correct point.

Read the student's work through once to get an overall view of their response.

Focus on general points
☐ Did it make sense?
☐ Did it flow?
☐ Did the story arouse any feeling?
☐ Did you want to read on? Was the description interesting?
☐ Was the handwriting readable?

Now focus on the detail. Read each of the following points and find out whether the student's work has these features.

Focus on content
☐ Did the opening sentence(s) 'grab' the reader's interest?
☐ Was the setting established (i.e. when and where the action took place)?
☐ Was it apparent who the main character(s) is/are?
☐ Have personal pronouns been used?
☐ Did descriptions make reference to any of the senses? (e.g. *soft grass*)
☐ Were interesting details included?

☐ Did the conclusion have a satisfactory summing-up comment?

Focus on structure, vocabulary, grammar, spelling, punctuation
☐ Was there a variation in sentence length and beginnings?
☐ Was there a new paragraph started for changes in time, place or action?
☐ Were adjectives used to improve descriptions? (e.g. <u>majestic</u> trees)
☐ Were adverbs used to make actions more interesting? (e.g. *walked* <u>briskly</u>)
☐ Were capital letters used where they should have been?
☐ Was punctuation correct?
☐ Was the spelling of words correct?

Marker's suggestions (optional)

LITERACY – LANGUAGE CONVENTIONS   Pages 111–114

1 laundry **2** careful **3** wives **4** lunches
5 wired **6** ledge **7** window **8** centre
9 hasty **10** envelope **11** alarm **12** face
13 green **14** minute **15** people **16** warned
17 would **18** and **19** struck **20** lashed
21 of **22** use **23** summer **24** lie **25** too
26 A **27** D **28** B **29** C **30** C **31** A, D **32** D
33 A **34** B **35** B **36** C **37** A **38** D **39** C **40** D
41 B **42** C **43** B, C **44** A **45** A **46** C **47** A
48 B **49** A **50** C

EXPLANATIONS

1 The correct spelling is *laundry*, not 'laundery'. Tip: Make sure you pronounce the word correctly. The sound at the end of the word is 'ry' not 'ery'.

2 The correct spelling is *useful,* not 'usefull'. Tip: When the suffix *full* is added to a word, one letter *l* is dropped (e.g. *useful, hopeful*).

3 The correct spelling is *wives*, not 'wifes'.
Tip: To make the plural of many words which end in *f* or *fe*, the *f* changes to *v* and *es* is added (*life—lives, half—halves*).

4 The correct spelling is *lunches*, not 'lunchers'.
Tip: Make sure you pronounce the word correctly—*lunches* not 'lunchers'. To make the plural form of words ending in *ch*, add *es*—not just the *s* (*bunch—bunches*).

5 The correct spelling is *wired*, not 'wird'.
Tip: The *ed* ending is added to most words when used as past tense. As *wire* ends with an *e*, we simply add *d*.

6 The correct spelling is *ledge*, not 'legde'.
Tip: The letters *g* and *d* have swapped positions. Take care not to reverse letter order: *dge* is a common word ending. Learn to recognise word groups with similar spellings (e.g. *edge, wedge, lodge*).

7 The correct spelling is *window*, not 'winder'.
Tip: Make sure you pronounce the word carefully. Both *er* and *ow* are common letter combinations in words. Learn to recognise word groups with similar spellings (e.g. *willow, finder*).

8 The correct spelling is *centre*, not *center*.
Tip: *Center* is the American spelling. There are a number of words with the *re* ending which sounds like the *er* ending (*metre, theatre*). Learn to recognise word groups with similar spellings.

9 The correct spelling is *hasty*, not 'hastey'.
Tip: When adding *y* to words that end with a consonant + *e* it is common to drop the *e* before adding the *y*. Learn to recognise the spelling of common words with similar spelling (e.g. *wire—wiry, taste—tasty*).

10 The correct spelling is *envelope*, not 'envelop'.
Tip: Make sure you pronounce the word correctly. The word ends with *lope*, not *lop*.

11 The correct spelling is *alarm,* not 'arlarm'.
Tip: Make sure you pronounce the word correctly. The correct word is *alarm*.

12 The correct spelling is *face*, not 'fase'.
Tip: Learn to recognise word groups with similar spellings (e.g. *race, place*).

13 The correct spelling is *green*, not 'grene'.
Tip: Both *een* and *ene* sound the same. Learn to recognise word groups that go together (*seen, teen; gene, scene*). The *ene* spelling is much less common in short words.

14 The correct spelling is *minute*, not 'minet'.
Tip: *Minute* is a common word and one you have to know.

15 The correct spelling is *people*.
Tip: The letters *o* and *e* have swapped positions. Take care not to reverse letter order. *People* is a common word you should learn to spell.

16 The misspelled word is *warned*.
Tip: The word sounds as if it should have a different spelling. The *war* in *warned* has the same pronunciation as in *war* (battle).

17 The misspelled word is *would*.
Tip: Learn the different spellings of words that sound the same. *Wood* refers to timber and *would* suggests something might happen. Learn when to use them correctly.

18 The misspelled word is *and*.
Tip: Make sure you pronounce the word correctly. *And* is a joining word. The *end* is the last part.

19 The misspelled word is *struck*.
Tip: The ending *uck* is much more common than the *uk* ending. Learn to recognise word groups with similar spellings (e.g. *truck, buck*).

20 The misspelled word is *lashed*.
Tip: Make sure you pronounce the word correctly. The *t* sound is incorrect.

㉑ The misspelled word is *of*.
Tip: *Of* and *off* sound a little bit similar. Make sure you pronounce the word correctly.

㉒ The misspelled word is *use*.
Tip: *Use* is a common word and one you have to know. Don't confuse it with *yours*.

㉓ The misspelled word is *summer*.
Tip: Make sure you pronounce the word correctly. The letters *er* and *ar* can sound the same on the end of words. The *er* is more often at the end of words (*faster*, *runner*).

㉔ The misspelled word is *lie*.
Tip: Don't confuse certain common words that rhyme with *lie* and have a similar spelling (*dye*, *bye*).

㉕ The misspelled word is *too*.
Tip: Learn the different spellings of words that sound the same, in this case *too* (meaning 'more than necessary') and *to* (indicating a place). These are common words and easy to misuse.

㉖ This is a grammar question. The correct word is *hers*.
Tip: *Her* (as does *mine*) contains the meaning of ownership (*her dress*). It is not necessary to add the apostrophe *s* to show ownership. *Her* is incorrect because it simply stands for Beth. *She's* is short for *she is*.

㉗ This is a grammar question. The correct word is *dug*.
Tip: *Dug* is an irregular verb. Most verbs in English form their past tenses by adding *ed* (e.g. *he walked*). There are a number of irregular verbs when this doesn't happen. We say *dug* instead of 'digged' (or 'dugged'). *Dig* could only be used if there was more than one dog—*the dogs dig …*

㉘ This is a grammar question. The correct answer is *have written*.
Tip: With the verb *written* you need the correct 'helper'—another verb to 'help' it. *Have*, *has* and *had* can be helping verbs. The

correct verb is *have* because there is more than one person (*we*) writing the invitation. *Has written* would be correct for one person —*Stan has written …*

㉙ This is a grammar question. The correct word is *later*.
Tip: In this sentence, *later* refers to the time after right now. *Soon* refers to a time not too distant into the future.

㉚ This is a grammar question. The correct word is the pronoun *which*.
Tip: *Which* is used for animals and things. A *river* is a thing. When referring to people, you use *who*. *What* is used for questions.

㉛ This is a punctuation question. The correct answer is: *On Tuesday, Len is four(.) I am not four until next week but Sara is already five(.)*
Tip: There are two statements so there must be two full stops. Each sentence starts with a capital letter. The second sentence starts with *I*. The first full stop goes at the end of the first sentence, after *four*. The second full stop goes at the end of the second sentence, after *five*.

㉜ This is a grammar question. The correct word is *along*.
Tip: *Along* is used when there is progress from one point to another (*gate* to *shed*). *On* does not suggest movement. *Into* involves going inside.

㉝ This is a punctuation question. The correct word is *led*.
Tip: *Led* is an irregular verb. Most verbs in English form their past tenses by adding *ed* (e.g. *he walked*). There are a number of irregular verbs when this doesn't happen. We say *led* instead of 'leaded'. *Lead* could only be used if there was more than one knight—*the knights lead … Lead* (sounding like *led*) also has the meaning of the soft grey metal.

㉞ This is a grammar question. The correct word is *into*.

Tip: It is common usage to say *into battle*. *Onto* would be used if the sentence contained *onto the battlefield*.

35 This is a punctuation question. The correct word is *victory.* (with a full stop).
Tip: The next sentence starts with a capital letter (*Did*). There has to be a full stop after *victory*. As it is a statement, it needs a full stop.

36 This is a punctuation question. The correct sentence is: *Did he ever get injured?*
Tip: Questions often start with *did*, *is* or *was*. The question mark goes at the end of the question: *Did he ever get injured?*

37 This is a grammar question. The correct word is *fell*.
Tip: *Fell* is an irregular verb. Most verbs in English form their past tenses by adding *ed* (e.g. *he walked*). There are a number of irregular verbs when this doesn't happen. We say *fell* instead of 'falled' (or 'felled'). If *fallen* is used it must have a helper: *had* (*had fallen*).

38 This is a grammar question. The correct word is *and*.
Tip: *And* is a conjunction joining two similar things. *An* is incorrect (it is an indefinite article and is used before words beginning with a vowel sound).

39 This is a punctuation question. The correct sentence is: *Australia Day celebrations are held in January every year.*
Tip: The word *year* is a common noun in this sentence. It does not need a capital letter. The words *Australia Day* and *January* are proper nouns and have capital letters.

40 This is a punctuation question. The correct sentence is: *The captain's orders were to pass all flags to the leaders.*
Tip: The orders are the captain's orders. Captain has to have an apostrophe *s* ('*s*). There is no need for an apostrophe *s* with *flags, orders* or *leaders* as no ownership is involved.

41 This is a grammar question. The correct word is *a*.
Tip: The word *black* begins with a consonant so we say *a black*. *An* goes before words starting with vowels.

42 This is a grammar question. The correct word is *along*.
Tip: Prepositions show the position of something in place or in time. The preposition *along* indicates that the tourists are moving over the length of the cliff track.

43 This is a punctuation question. The correct sentence is: *Can we borrow books (,) CDs (,) magazines and posters from the town library?*
Tip: Commas (,) suggest that there should be a pause and are used to show separate different items in the question: Can we borrow books, CDs, magazines ... The word *and* is used to separate the last two items and no comma is required.

44 This is a punctuation question. The correct sentence is: *The teacher said, "Is two plus two really five?"*
Tip: The teacher asks a question. A question mark is required after the last word the teacher says and is placed inside the inverted commas (?"). The teacher's question must start with a capital letter (*Is*).

45 This is a grammar question. The unnecessary words are *a question*.
Tip: To *ask* is to pose a question, so *a question* is redundant or unnecessary. No meaning is lost by omitting *a question*.

46 This is a grammar question. The correct sentence is: *The cat and the dog are good friends.*
Tip: **Basic rule:** Singular subjects (nouns) need singular verbs; plural subjects (nouns) need plural verbs. Use *are* when talking about more than two things. In this sentence *are* must be used because there are two animals that are friends.

47 This is a grammar question. The correct sentence is: *Jack has his painting. Whose is this one?*
Tip: There are two parts: *Jack has his painting.* is a statement and ends with a full stop. The question starts with the word *Whose* and ends with a question mark (?). *Who* doesn't own the book so you can't use *who's book*. *Who's* is not a contraction for *who is*. *He's* is short for *he is*.

48 This is a grammar question. The correct word is *best*.
Tip: Use *est* words (best) when comparing more than two items. When comparing two items use words ending in *er* (*better*). There would be more than one player in the street.
Remember: *good, better, best*. One player is *good*, he is *better* than another player and he is the *best* of many players.

49 This is a grammar question. The correct word is *anymore*.
Tip: The word *anymore* is a compound word. It is an adverb and does not take a capital.

50 This is a grammar question. The correct word is *was*.
Tip: **Basic rule:** Singular subjects (nouns) need singular verbs; plural subjects (nouns) need plural verbs. We use *was* when talking about a single person or thing. In this sentence *was* must be used because *I* refers to just one person: *I was silent.*

LITERACY – READING   Pages 115–121

Snowflakes

1 B   2 A   3 D   4 C   5 D   6 B

EXPLANATIONS

1 Krystal is catching snowflakes. Jasper is the boy from next door.

2 Kystal's father was being tricky. No two snowflakes are the same.

3 Another good title: Krystal Gets Conned. Krystal didn't realise she was given an impossible task. The passage is not about a snowman. Jasper is doubtful but this is not as important as Krystal being conned. The twenty snowflakes is just a minor detail.

4 A snowflake has six points. The first two Kyrstal looked at have six arms 'like you see in pictures'.

5 For some questions you have to combine the facts that you read in the text with your own knowledge and observations. You have to use your knowledge of word meanings as they are used in the passage. Krystal felt angry. She glared at the house.

6 Jasper admitted he couldn't make a snowman stand up. His snowmen always fell over.

Blue Tongue Lizard

7 A   8 C   9 D   10 written response   11 C   12 A
EXPLANATIONS

7 The mouth of a blue Tongue Lizard is pink. The tongue is blue. The other colours are body colours.

8 Bask means to enjoy lying in the sun. For some questions you will have to combine the facts that you read in the text with your own knowledge and observations.

9 The passage does not say that the Blue Tongue eats birds' eggs. According to the passage, the Blue Tongue eats plant matter and invertebrates (animals without backbones).

10 The palest part of the Blue Tongue's skin is the belly.

11 Blue Tongues have strong jaw muscles. Blue Tongues have small eyes and short legs.

12 The Blue Tongue lizard scares predators by sticking out its tongue.

Knock-down Clown

13 D **14** B **15** A **16** C **17** B **18** D

EXPLANATIONS

13 For some questions you will have to combine the facts that you read in the text with your own knowledge and observations. These instructions could be part of a science experiment because you are experimenting with the centre of gravity of an object.

14 Craft knives are sharp and can be dangerous. It is best to ask an adult to cut the ball in half.

15 The scissors are used to trim the paper tube. You keep trimming the tube until it works properly.

16 Because the clown has a low centre of gravity it returns to an upright position if pushed.

17 The coloured pencils are used to decorate the tube (by drawing a clown on it).

18 It is best to make the paper tube lighter by trimming off some of the paper.

Kangaroo Paw

19 A **20** C **21** A **22** B **23** D **24** C **25** B

EXPLANATIONS

19 The hairs on the Kangaroo Paw do trap water.

20 A floral emblem is a badge design based upon flowers. For some questions you have to combine the facts that you read in the text with your own knowledge and observations.

21 Birds pollinate all types of Kangaroo Paws. Some are pollinated by bees and some by small mammals.

22 The Kangaroo Paw is unusual because it has no smell (unscented).

23 The flower looks like a star. You have to look at the picture of the Kangaroo Paw.

24 The stem is red.

25 Kangaroo Paws grow well in sandy soil.

Circus Poster

26 D **27** A **28** A **29** B **30** C **31** D

EXPLANATIONS

26 26th (January) – a Saturday.

27 The ladies are doing a balancing act. This information is in the picture.

28 $20 (A family going to the matinee would pay half price ($40 ÷ 2)).

29 The stilt waker also has a juggling act. This information is written on the poster.

30 The clown has a balancing act. This information is written on the poster.

31 The poster is intended to convince people to go to the circus—not join the circus. The poster is not for sale.

The Computer Swallowed Grandpa

32 C **33** 4, 1, 3, 2 **34** B **35** D **36** A **37** C

EXPLANATIONS

32 Grandpa disappeared when he pressed 'control' and 'enter'.

33 This is a sequencing type of question. By reading the text carefully you can identify the correct order of events.

34 A tribute is words of praise. For some questions you will have to combine the facts that you read in the text with your own knowledge and observations. You have to use your knowledge of word meanings as they are used in the passage.

35 The poet's feelings towards grandparents is one of respect. For some questions you will have to combine the facts that you read in the text with your own knowledge and observations.

36 The poet tried Google because he had run out of ideas to find Grandpa. For some questions you will have to combine the facts that you read in the text with your own knowledge.

37 The poem is a plea for help to find Grandpa.

CONFUSION

38 B **39** written response **40** D

EXPLANATIONS

38 Sally doesn't know why her mother asked the question, she didn't see the parade.

39 Sally only saw legs (second frame).

40 The bubbles are used in cartoons and comics to show what a person is thinking (remembering).

NUMERACY   Pages 122–126

1 B 2 C 3 A 4 C 5 B 6 76 7 A 8 A 9 A 10 B
11 D 12 C 13 C 14 C 15 20 16 B 17 C 18 D 19 B
20 D 21 7 22 A 23 D 24 8541 25 B 26 10 27 C
28 11 29 3.85 30 A 31 22 32 C 33 14 34 12 35 B

EXPLANATIONS

1 The mass of a mobile phone would be about 120 grams.

2

3 Peter used these coins to total $2.80:

4 A pentagon has 5 sides:

5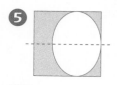

6 45 + 31 = 45 + 30 + 1
= 75 + 1
= 76

7 When completely covered, the grid would contain 8 stickers. As there are already 2 stickers on the grid, Jessie needs another 6 stickers.

8 12 × 4 = 48.
Consider each of the choices:
24 × 2 = 48   This is the correct answer
6 × 6 = 36
8 × 10 = 80
6 × 4 = 24

9 Now 15 + 14 = 15 + 10 + 4
= 25 + 4
= 29
Also, 33 – 'what number' is 29.
The number is 4 as 33 – 4 = 29

10 From 5:15 to 5:35 is 20 minutes. If the lesson runs for 30 minutes, Riley has another 10 minutes remaining.

11 When multiplying by 5, the answer will have a last digit of 0 or 5. This means that 53 will not be an answer.

12 If the bag of balls cost $2, then we can find the number of balls by dividing:
No. of bags = 10 ÷ 2
= 5
Now the 5 bags contain 3 balls each:
No. of balls = 5 × 3
= 15
The number of balls is 15.

13 From P, move 1 square down to I, then 2 squares left to K and then 2 squares up to W.

14 An octagon inside a hexagon is an 8 sided figure inside a 6-sided figure:

15. Emily walked 8 laps and Grace walked 12 laps.
Total = 8 + 12
= 20
The girls walked a total of 20 laps.

16. The 16 buttons are arranged in 4 rows. As 16 ÷ 4 = 4, there will be 4 buttons in each new row.

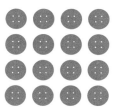

17. There are 4 rows of squares, so Aleksi needs to shade 3 of the 4 rows.
By counting, Aleksi needs to shade another 15 squares.

18. Now remove the same objects from both sides of the balance:

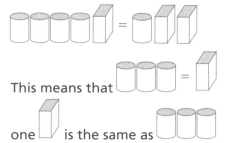

19. Fleur is sitting in the first row, second from the right.

20. By shading every 3rd square, Yvette would shade number 54.
Another method is to continue the shading pattern:

1	2	3	4	5	6	7	8	9	10
11	12	13	14	15	16	17	18	19	20
21	22	23	24	25	26	27	28	29	30
31	32	33	34	35	36	37	38	39	40
41	42	43	44	45	46	47	48	49	50
51	52	53	54	55	56	57	58	59	60

21. Using the key, 1 symbol = 2 students and $\frac{1}{2}$ symbol = 1 student.
As the car has $3\frac{1}{2}$ symbols, then
3 × 2 + 1 = 7.
This means 7 students came to school by car.

22. When this shape is rotated a quarter of a turn in the clockwise direction:

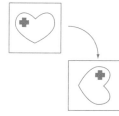

23. Each apple can be cut into 4 quarters. Half an apple can be cut into 2 quarters. This gives a total of 14 quarters.

24. First arrange the number from highest to lowest: 8, 5, 4, 1. The largest number is formed by using the numbers in the order from highest to lowest. The largest possible number is 8541.

25. As $79 is closer to **$80** than $70 and $43 is closer to **$40** than $50, the best estimate is $80 + $40.

26. To make 6 cupcakes she uses 4 marshmallows. This means for every 3 cupcakes she uses 2 marshmallows. If we multiply both numbers by 5, we get 15 cupcakes that need 10 marshmallows.

27. 1086 = 1 × 1000 + 8 × 10 + 6 × 1
= One thousand and eighty six

28. Half of $32 is $16. If the difference in the two prices is $10, then the wallet is $5 more than $16 and the key ring is $5 less than $16. This means that the key ring cost $11.

29. We need to add $2.25 and $1.60. $2 and $1 is $3 and 25 and 60 is 85. This means Suzie started with $3.85.

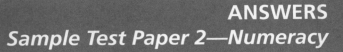
30 The least likely colour is red as it has the smallest area on the spinner.

31 From 8:50 to 9:00 is 10 minutes. Then to 9:12 is another 12 minutes. This gives a total of 22 minutes.

32 There are 2 columns shaded out of the 5 columns. This means a fraction of $\frac{2}{5}$.

33 Each of the 4 layers has 6 boxes. This means 24 boxes will fit into the carton. By counting we have 10 boxes in the carton already. This means another 14 boxes can fit into the carton.

34 The total of the three cards is 2 + 3 + 4 = 9. If Mitchell's total is 36, then he must have 4 of each of the cards. As 4 lots of 3 makes 12, then Mitchell has 12 cards on the table.

35 Add each girl's daily totals:
Juilet: 3 + 6 + 6 + 4 + 3 = 22
Tara: 4 + 4 + 8 + 7 + 6 = 29
Sophie: 6 + 7 + 5 + 6 + 4 = 28
Ella: 6 + 7 + 5 + 6 + 4 = 28
Tara received the most emails.